BACK FROM THE BRINK

BACK
FROM
THE
BRINK

A Family Guide to
Overcoming Traumatic Stress

Don R. Catherall, Ph.D.

Produced by Cathy D. Hemming and
The Philip Lief Group, Inc.

BANTAM BOOKS
NEW YORK • TORONTO • LONDON • SYDNEY • AUCKLAND

BACK FROM THE BRINK

A Bantam Book / June 1992

Library of Congress Cataloging-in-Publication Data

Catherall, Donald Roy, 1946–
    Back from the brink: a family guide to overcoming traumatic
stress / Don R. Catherall.
        p.   cm.
    Includes index.
    ISBN 0-553-08977-3
    1. Post-traumatic stress disorder.   2. Psychic trauma.   3. Post-
traumatic stress disorder—Patients—Family relationships.   I. Title.
    RC552.P67C38   1992
    616.85′21—dc20   91-32405
                                                                                CIP

Published simultaneously in the United States and Canada

Bantam Books are published by Bantam Books, a division of Bantam
Doubleday Dell Publishing Group, Inc. Its trademark, consisting of the
words "Bantam Books" and the portrayal of a rooster, is Registered in
U.S. Patent and Trademark Office and in other countries. Marca
Registrada. Bantam Books, 666 Fifth Avenue, New York, New York
10103.

PRINTED IN THE UNITED STATES OF AMERICA

BVG   0 9 8 7 6 5 4 3 2 1

Toward the end of World War II, my father suffered a series of traumas on Tarawa, Iwo Jima, and other islands in the Pacific. He was later wounded on Okinawa. And my mother, while still a child, lost her mother to a major illness. So I know what it is to grow up in a family where people have been traumatized. I married a woman who also knows what it's like to grow up in such a family: Her father was the sole survivor of the bridge on a U.S. destroyer that was hit by a kamikaze plane three days before the war ended. Over the years I've come to appreciate the ubiquitous nature of trauma; many, many families have been exposed, and even people who weren't present when a trauma occurred are affected by it. Once a trauma touches a family, its effects seep down through the generations.

This book is dedicated to the children. We heal ourselves because we owe it to them.

Humpty Dumpty sat on a wall,
Humpty Dumpty took a great fall;
All the king's horses and all the king's men
Couldn't put Humpty together again.
. . . It was time to get the family involved.

CONTENTS

        Through, Reconnecting, and Moving On   221
12 Seeking Professional Help: Finding the Right
        Therapist and the Right Treatment   239

    Afterword   255
    Appendix: Resources   261
    Index   265

ACKNOWLEDGMENTS

There are three groups of people I wish to acknowledge as making this book possible. The first is my family: my wife, my daughter, and my son. I always thought writers thanked their families because of the moral support they received while writing, but it's much more than that. They sacrificed the most valuable thing we have, family time. Thank you, Kim, Kate, and Cody.

The second group I wish to thank consists of the people who gave me editorial help. They were Linda Lowenthal and Maria Mack at Bantam, and elsewhere, Cathy Hemming and, most of all, the indomitable Nancy Kalish. Nancy's spirit is uplifting, I hope this book conveys the spirit she infused into this project. They all provided tremendous support and encouragement by believing in the importance of this topic. They are also skillful editors who helped me organize my thoughts more coherently.

The final, and most important, group that I must thank is the people who shared their personal traumas with me—my clients. It is these individuals and families who've taught me the most about traumatization and recovery.

BACK FROM THE BRINK

INTRODUCTION

Most of us have had traumatic experiences in our lives. Usually, we're upset for a while, but eventually we get over them and life continues. But occasionally, some of us run into events that are so traumatic that we can't get over them without help. We still hurt and reexperience the trauma long after normal grieving should have ended. When this happens, we've not only been exposed to a painful experience, we've been traumatized by it. We feel decidedly abnormal and it may be quite some time before we come to feel normal again.

This process is the *trauma response*. It includes not only the unpleasant experiences that we think of as traumatization but the period of healing and recovering from the traumatization as well.

Various symptoms can follow a trauma. Some call these symptoms a disorder, even a disease. But whatever the name, these symptoms are a normal response to an abnormal experience. Like a scab that forms over a wound, a psychological trauma heals underneath a protective membrane that must eventually peel away. A large part of that protective membrane is made up of supportive relationships with people who understand that the wound may not be visible but that the processes of hurting and healing—and the need for helping—are very real.

The duration, intensity, and severity of the trauma response varies with the individual. Some people are traumatized by things that don't seem to leave much impact on others. But once the trauma response begins in a person, it must run its course. If the process becomes blocked, the person stays traumatized. And the trauma response is not limited to the individual who was exposed to the trauma; it includes the people who are involved with that person. Those loved ones become part of the process, both the hurting and the healing.

Once you have been traumatized, you live in a world that's different from that of other people. The people who care about you will notice the change and try to help. But friends and family often don't know how to help. Loving and living with someone who has been traumatized can pull the helper into the survivor's traumatized world. As a result, the helpers can actually become traumatized themselves.

This book was written to help those people who have lived through the trauma directly and those who lived through it indirectly, through being the loved ones of a trauma survivor. My goal is twofold: to reach those who have been traumatized and help them learn to use their relationships with family and loved ones to overcome their outer isolation and inner turmoil; and to provide family or loved ones with tools to facilitate the natural healing process and help them in their daily task of staying emotionally involved with the person who is traumatized.

Post-traumatic Stress Disorder

Modern society's awareness of the lasting effects of traumatization stems primarily from the people who have been psychologically damaged in our century's wars and in the Holocaust. Traumatized combat veterans have been described with terms like *shell shock*, *battle fatigue*, and *combat neurosis*. Holocaust survivors were viewed as suffering from the aftereffects of such profound mistreatment as torture, degradation, loss, and dehumanization. Yet despite public awareness of groups such as these, the psychiatric community did not widely acknowledge the lasting psychological damage produced by traumatization until the late 1970s, when the diagnosis of Post-traumatic Stress Disorder (PTSD) was introduced.

At that time, many of the traumatized veterans of the Vietnam War had gone undiagnosed for over a decade. Those who had sought help were frequently misdiagnosed, often being viewed as suffering from character or personality problems; their complaints about the effects of their war experience were frequently discounted. Their bizarre hallucinatory flashbacks even led some of them to be given extreme psychiatric diagnoses—such as schizophrenia—and to be treated with antipsychotic and sedating drugs.

In the 1980s, there was a sudden wave of interest in traumatization. I was involved in the Vietnam veterans' movement, and much of my own understanding of PTSD stems from that work. But what I have to say about traumatization does not apply only to war veterans or to Holocaust survivors. It's for *everyone* who's been traumatized, regardless of the specific nature of the trauma. Every trauma has its own unique meaning, but there is an underlying common structure to everyone's trauma response.

The Sources of Traumatic Stress

Once we understood that the symptoms of Vietnam veterans were the result of traumatization, we began to recognize this syndrome in people with many other types of trauma. This awareness was brought home to me when I was working with a group of parents whose children had been physically and sexually abused by someone outside the family. As I listened to the parents talk, I realized that they sounded exactly like a group of Vietnam veterans. They couldn't escape what had happened; it seemed to follow them around every day. They felt alienated from society, as if there were a wall between them and other people. They viewed people outside that wall as naive and superficial, not terribly concerned about the agony of their family. Their former friends seemed to have lost interest in these people as their traumatization dragged on for years.

That feeling of being different from other people is common to people who have experienced traumas related to war, to violent crime, to physical and sexual abuse, to life in an alcoholic family, to accidents and disasters, and to chronic and terminal illnesses. Each of these categories includes not only many different traumas, but many different ways in which people are related to the traumas. For instance, war traumas include not only those of combatants in the war zone, but also those of Holocaust survivors and their descendents, people who have been tortured, people who have lived in concentration camps or as prisoners of war, civilians in the war zone, military and civilian personnel who were exposed to the casualties of war, and the families and loved ones of all of these people.

Violent crimes—such as homicide, assault, rape, suicide, and terrorism—affect police, hospital personnel, and others who deal with trauma victims and their loved ones. People who live in abusive situations—battered wives, molested children, violent families—may leave the abusive situation itself but take the fears into their new families and create distrust. And the children raised in that atmosphere of distrust will be affected by their parents' traumatization.

Throughout history, natural disasters (earthquakes, floods, fires, tornadoes, hurricanes, plagues, droughts), manmade disasters (shipwrecks, plane/train/auto accidents, and nuclear and other industrial accidents), and chronic and terminal illnesses (leprosy, cancer, AIDS) have traumatized people and those who cared for them.

We've all been at least on the periphery of a trauma. Even people whose personal lives have been surprisingly free of trauma have still been affected by more distant events. We are all affected by things that happen to our community, whether local, regional, national, or global. Most Americans felt personally affected when President Kennedy was assassinated, when the *Challenger* blew up, or when Hurricane Hugo devastated the South Carolina coast. If we perceive ourselves as part of the community that suffers a traumatic event, we experience that trauma on a personal level too. As human beings, we feel affected by earthquakes that destroy communities on the other side of the world.

When You Are Affected

Although you've probably experienced many such community traumatic events, you probably weren't personally traumatized by them. But you or your loved one may have experienced a personal trauma. You may find an example of that trauma in this book, but you might not, since the examples in the book represent only *some* of the things that people experience as traumatic.

What constitutes a traumatic experience is, to a degree, a subjective affair. If you feel personally damaged by the experience, then for you it was traumatic. This is similar to the way people experience pain; some people can bear much more than others. Moreover, your feelings of devastation and hopelessness from a traumatic event depend upon the *meaning* you give that event. A trauma can produce a state of traumatization in one person and not in another because it holds a different meaning for each person.

It's important to distinguish between *trauma* and *traumatization*. Everyone encounters trauma, but not everyone is traumatized. Traumas are relatively common life experiences, and there are well-established mechanisms that we use to cope with the traumas we encounter. Some of those mechanisms work better than others, and some work better for some people than for others. People are traumatized when the effects of a trauma continue to disrupt or control their life, even though the effects may be buried for years before they emerge.

Five factors are involved in determining whether you'll be traumatized by an event. The first three factors have to do with how you experience the event, they are: the meaning you give it, your personal characteristics, and the actual nature of the event. Two more factors are involved in how you *cope* with the traumatization, your personal coping skills and the kind of help you get from other people. This book is meant to help you improve your coping skills and the help you give in your relationships.

Being the loved one of a trauma survivor is not easy. He has unusual needs; he needs to draw into himself and examine the effects of the trauma on his feelings about himself and how he fits in the world. And at the same time he needs to feel connected and supported by caring people who understand him and what he's been through. You may find yourself trying to connect without imposing—a difficult balancing act.

For the trauma survivor, the natural healing process can become blocked, resulting in a breakdown in trust. When you don't trust people, you don't dare to open up. Healing normally goes on in a casual, everyday sort of way—between you and yourself and you and others. But nothing happens if you can't trust. When trust breaks down, therapy can serve as a catalyst for the natural healing to resume.

Identifying Traumatization

You may be wondering whether you or someone close to you has been traumatized. The definition of trauma is somewhat vague. Clearly, someone is likely to be traumatized when he or she has suffered an extreme life-threatening experience, such as a bad car accident or a wartime experience. But people often describe non-life-threatening experiences as traumatic, such as a vicious divorce, an unexpected financial disaster, or the premature death of a loved one.

What constitutes a trauma is not only the event, but how the individual interprets the event. If you're wondering whether you or someone you care about has been traumatized, here are some questions to consider.

If you think you may have been traumatized by an event
or events:

- Did some event interrupt and change your life for
  the worse?
- When you think about that event, do you feel pain,
  anxiety, rage, guilt, or grief? Or is there a curious
  lack of emotion when you would normally expect
  to feel something?
- Has there been a decline in the quality of your life
  since the event, either immediately after or at
  some later point?
- Are you frequently reminded of the event? Does it
  occupy your mind more than you think it should?
- Have you become isolated, less involved with
  other people than you were in the past?
- Do you find it very difficult to trust people?
- Are you troubled about what happened, still trying to figure out how you may have caused it or
  handled it differently?
- Do you think about the possibility of it happening
  again?
- Do you find that you are emotionally numb, unaffected by events that you know are disturbing to
  other people?
- Do you have sleep problems? Have you ever re-
  sorted to drinking or working yourself to exhaustion in order to get to sleep?
- Does your life-style expose you to frequent risks?
- Do you feel you're different from other people,
  that you don't really fit in?
- Do you get depressed, have a drug or alcohol
  problem, or have problems maintaining your self-
  esteem?

If you think your loved one may have been traumatized:

- Do you know of some traumatic event that she lived through that may have affected her?

- Does some period or part of his life seem to lack detail or be missing altogether—leading you to wonder if something happened then that left a mark?

- Does she now talk as though her life is defined in terms of before and after the event?

- Does he seem to have curious attitudes about talking about it? Does it always come up in conversation? Or does it never come up, no matter how close the conversation veers to the subject?

- Does she leave you with a troubled feeling when she talks about the trauma, perhaps because distressing things are being said in a very unemotional manner, or perhaps because she appears to be struggling to control a great deal of emotion?

- Has he changed? Is he more volatile and difficult, or more withdrawn and distant?

- Do you feel that she no longer trusts you?

- Has the quality of your relationship changed? Is there an emotional gulf between you? Have you lost that connectedness that is the essence of a healthy relationship?

- Do you find yourself being pulled in different directions, wanting to spend time with her, yet finding that time to be so draining that you want to be away from her?

- Do you find yourself preoccupied with thoughts of what happened to him?

If you answered yes to more than half of the questions in either category, you or your loved one may have been traumatized. In Chapter 1 of this book, you'll learn the specific symptoms of Post-traumatic Stress Disorder (PTSD), and in Chapter 2 you'll learn more about the everyday experience of living with the disorder. After reading those chapters, you will be in a better position to judge whether you or your loved one is living in a traumatized state and perhaps could use some help with the healing process. If so, this book can help you make good use of the healing resources that are available to you.

People often expect recovery to return them to the level of functioning they had before the trauma. But reestablishing that level of functioning is not the same as getting back to your old self. One painful lesson about trauma is that life is never quite the same again. Those of you who have been directly traumatized—and many of you who were indirectly affected—are forever changed. But change is a part of life, and sometimes the final outcome of a traumatization is actually for the better.

Organization of the Book

The book is divided into three parts; "Hurting," "Helping," and "Healing." Part I, "Hurting," has three chapters that describe traumatization—what it is, what it's like to have it and what it's like to be involved with someone who has it. A few technical ideas are introduced in this first part as well as in subsequent parts of the book. I've tried to present these ideas in plain English and not obscure them with jargon. When I resort to technical terms, I'll explain their meaning, and I hope they'll become a part of your vocabulary as you proceed through the book. Several important concepts—such as *processing a trauma*—reappear a number of times.

Part II of the book, "Helping," focuses on the process of overcoming the traumatization. Its first chapter gives an overview of the recovery process, while each of the others is directed to the various individuals involved: those who've been traumatized, those who are the loved ones of traumatized people, and the parents of traumatized children. Each chapter provides guidelines to aid you and your loved ones in helping each other.

Part III, "Healing," contains five chapters that focus on solutions to various problems and symptoms. They deal with physical symptoms (fatigue, stress, sleep problems), emotional symptoms (depression, anxiety, and reliance on alcohol/drugs), and interpersonal symptoms (isolation and poor self-esteem). Chapter 10 describes rituals that can facilitate the healing and it includes guidelines for families to create their own healing rituals. Chapter 11 identifies some deep-seated psychological issues that underlie the way many people respond to traumatization. It can help you make a more informed decision about whether to pursue psychotherapy. The last chapter offers assistance in finding the right kind of professional help for you or your traumatized loved one.

Using This Book

This book is intended to provide you with a clear feeling for what the trauma response is really like. If you're working on your own or a loved one's recovery, it helps enormously to have a feeling for what you are trying to make happen and to know what it feels like when you do it right. For that reason, I've included many case examples throughout the book. I've used pseudonyms and changed certain identifying details to protect the privacy of the people whose stories I share, but they are all real people. Although I worked with most of them in therapy, I haven't emphasized the therapy in my discussion—this isn't a book about therapy, it's about the natural healing process and how to maximize it.

I wrote this book because I saw there was a need for it. I've given workshops, seminars, and classes on the topic of trauma, but my audiences have generally been other professionals. Many of the things I say are commonsense, practical advice that families and others involved with a trauma survivor can follow. I want to make that advice directly available to you, the people who can actually put it to use. This book can help you improve your coping mechanisms and deal more effectively with both minor and major traumas, but it isn't intended to replace psychotherapy. It may augment it and, in some cases, perhaps make it unnecessary. Some traumatizations are too severe for you to expect to overcome them without professional help. Don't be reluctant to seek such help, especially if someone is seriously depressed or behaving in a dangerous manner, such as sounding suicidal or abusing drugs or alcohol.

I've chosen to work with trauma because of the people I've met in the field, both as clients and as colleagues. There seems to be a high incidence of personal trauma among the professionals who've chosen to specialize in this field, and they invariably possess a sense of duty and strong commitment. I'm proud to be a member of such a group. People who have been traumatized know that the emperor has no clothes. They have a great appreciation for the fragility of life, the vulnerability of each of us. Some of them are still victims. Successful recovery means no longer being a victim. It means being a survivor.

Part I

HURTING

1

A BROKEN LIFE
Traumatization and How It Happens

William served a year as an infantryman in Vietnam. Like
many men who see heavy combat, William experienced a
number of traumatic events. He lost several close friends, he
was nearly killed several times, and on one occasion he was
certain he was going to die. But he did make it home, and
once there he tried to put Vietnam behind him. He went to
college on the G.I. bill, but he didn't perform well; his concentration was poor and he couldn't apply himself to his
studies. He was preoccupied with Vietnam; memories of the
carnage kept coming back to him. He had some success at
forgetting Vietnam during the day, but at night it invaded his
dreams. In fact, it was hard to sleep because of recurring
nightmares. He was trying to live his life as though his experiences in Vietnam were nothing but history and therefore
had no further effect upon him.

Socially, he couldn't fit in with the other students, and
he lived a very isolated life. He worked at jobs that required a
minimum of dealing with people. He lived alone in a dilapi-

dated house outside town and spent less and less time interacting with the other students at the university. He'd hunted
as a boy, and now he kept weapons in his house and spent
long hours cleaning them. The only social life he had was
occasionally visiting bars in the area, where he sometimes
found himself talking to strangers about his experiences in
Vietnam. Still, he somehow kept up his grades and got by.

After about a year of this life, however, he started drinking too much, and his performance and his attendance at
school fell off. Finally, he gave up on school and went to
work full time as a security guard. But he lost that job because of frequent absences. After that, he drifted for several
years, holding a series of jobs. Eventually, he wound up at a
commune where everyone was into natural foods, yoga,
meditation, and other health-oriented pursuits. He found
that they accepted him as long as he did his share of the
work. Over a period of months, he stopped drinking and became a valued member of the commune.

William stayed at the commune for over five years. During that time he talked to people about his experience in
Vietnam. More than once, he got upset as he recalled some of
the things that most disturbed him. But the commune accepted him—they wanted to understand what he'd been
through. This gave William a sanctuary where he could examine what had happened to him and come to terms with
the emotional turmoil with which he'd been struggling.
Slowly, the turmoil subsided. As he regained his ability to
apply himself to projects, he apprenticed himself to two
members of the commune who taught him carpentry. Eventually, he fell in love and got married, and he and his wife left
the commune and moved to a city. Today William is a master
carpenter and a devoted family man.

William's story is not uncommon. Many Vietnam veterans came home and discovered that they couldn't fit into the
world they had left. They tried to resume the business of living the best they could. Some were lucky enough to find a
niche where they fit, but others were not so lucky. William's
story is one of the successful ones: During his five years on
the commune, he lived a life that allowed him to feel ac

cepted and understood while he negotiated the painful process of healing from his traumatization.

Many of William's fellow veterans had similar problems,
such as drinking and having trouble with relationships and
holding a job. But when they sought help, their problems
were usually seen as the result of basic character flaws, and
they were viewed as misfits. The people around these men
didn't recognize that they were reeling from the effects of
their war experiences.

Lynn was a middle-aged professional woman who lived
alone in a large city. She enjoyed her career and put a lot of
energy into it, gaining positions of authority and status. She
led an active social life and maintained many friendships and
interests. Frequently she got together with family and friends
and attended cultural events and played sports. She liked the
city and had never been afraid of living there. All this
changed, however, after she was mugged.

Although the mugging lasted only a few seconds, Lynn
fought back and nearly got herself hurt very badly. After it
was over, Lynn tried to forget it and go on with her life as if
everything were normal again, but she found that she was
now afraid of many things. She didn't go out much, and she
lost contact with many of her friends. She stopped participating in sports and attending cultural events. Work was no
longer satisfying to her. Preoccupied with what had happened to her, she often relived the mugging in her mind,
always wary of it happening again. She found it increasingly difficult to sleep, and she started drinking to help her
sleep.

Lynn was traumatized by her experience. Fortunately,
she is a strong woman. Her life continues, and she does not
appear to be in a state of shock like some people who've been
traumatized. Most of the people she works with don't know
what she has been through. But inside, she feels different
from everyone else. She is no longer involved with people as
she once was; she feels very vulnerable around others. Despite the progress she has made, she hasn't reached the point
of feeling carefree again.

There are many similarities between William and Lynn. They were both traumatized by a near-death experience, despite the difference in magnitude. William was exposed to death almost daily for a year; Lynn had one brief—but intimate—brush with it. And they were affected in very similar ways: Both were traumatized, and both suffered from PTSD.

The Nature of Trauma

We all start out life totally dependent upon our caretakers to keep us alive and free of hurt, whether physical or emotional. In order to function independently, we slowly develop and learn to take care of ourselves. But a core feeling of extreme vulnerability stays with us, usually buried deep inside our memories. We learn to protect ourselves from feeling vulnerable by increasing our control over our environment and by convincing ourselves that we're safe.

Sometimes we aren't really as safe as we wish we were, so we fool ourselves by developing illusions of security. These illusions allow us to contend with the daily tasks of life without being constantly overwhelmed by anxiety about our underlying fragility. Periodically, however, things happen that remind us that we're not really as safe as we would like to think. We get hurt: Our bodies are torn, bones get broken, we get burned, or someone makes us feel unloved, uncared for, or worthless.

We've all experienced events that threaten our sense of safety. Those who are fortunate profited from those traumatic experiences. They developed strength of character, they learned that they could survive and that they could recover from fearful experiences. In effect, they became less controlled by their fears. But those less fortunate became more controlled by those fears. Perhaps they learned that they weren't as strong or as secure as they believed. They began to live in fear of more trauma, and their range of choices in life narrowed as a result.

Some traumas are immense, while others are relatively

minor—but all can be traumatizing. We expect an accident victim who has lost a limb to be traumatized, but we don't expect it from the bystander who only witnessed the accident. Yet traumas that appear to be minor can produce severe consequences, and sometimes those that seem to be major don't produce the catastrophic effects upon the individual that one would expect.

As I outlined in the introduction, our response to traumatic events is determined by five factors, including: (1) the nature of the event, (2) the meaning we give it, (3) our unique personality, (4) our coping style (this includes the way we learned to deal with past trauma), and (5) the nature of the response we get from others following our traumatic experiences.

From Trauma to Traumatization

The greatest difficulty we have in identifying traumatization is that we don't always know the meaning that a particular event has had for an individual. If you are traumatized and other people don't recognize what has happened to you, then you are less likely to recognize it yourself. You may live alone with it, with no opportunity to share your grief with others, or to talk about it and examine what it has done to you. It can be hard to recognize when someone has been traumatized because people are often *exposed* to trauma without being traumatized. We're accustomed to the idea that traumas are part of life, and that most of us deal with them at one time or another.

Images of Traumatization

Throughout history, individuals have been psychologically damaged as a result of their exposure to traumas. Stories of these individuals appear in our literature, our histories, and our cultural myths. One of the most common themes is the lone survivor of a cataclysm, such as a battle, a

sunken ship, a disease, or another natural disaster that devastated a community. He is a tragic figure, generally unable
to experience joy and haunted by the memory of what happened. Often, he lives a kind of death trip, pushing his own
luck until fate causes him to rejoin his lost companions
through his own death. In other cases, the survivor devotes
his life to serving or possibly avenging his comrades. Many of
the heroes of popular literature are such survivors, like the
Lone Ranger and the Phantom, who devote their lives to
helping others.

Captain Ahab, the whaler in Herman Melville's famous
novel *Moby-Dick,* is a survivor who endangers others in his
headlong rush to test fate and seek revenge. But ultimately,
he rejoins his lost comrades—a common outcome in stories
about lone survivors. Some survivors seek to repeat their
trauma; in a sense, they're trying to master it. And sometimes they feel so guilty about surviving when others didn't
that they repeat the trauma in order to satisfy their guilt, and
they continue to repeat it until fate finally catches up with
them.

Another common literary figure of traumatization is the
individual who has lost her sense of herself as a person. She
is seen as helpless, drifting in the sway of forces greater than
herself. Lorena, who is kidnapped and traumatized by rene-
gades in Larry McMurtry's novel *Lonesome Dove,* is unable
to care for herself and must live apart from other people
while she rediscovers her connection to civilized people.
Newt, the little girl in the 1986 movie *Aliens,* is similarly
unable to relate to people after surviving the devastation of
the aliens. Both Lorena and Newt are able to recover their
connections to other people only after one caring person persists in trying to reach out and understand them.

Our culture is full of images of traumatization. We see
them in novels, movies, on television—even in comic books.
It's the victim who is still in a state of shock long after the
traumatic event, who can't describe the horror of what he
has experienced though it is evident in his frozen expression.
It's the soldier who can only stutter in answer to the assault-

ive questioning of General Patton. It's the cold, single-minded heroine who has witnessed a villain kill her family. But are these cultural images truly representative of what trauma victims are like? The answer is—not entirely. These images are dramatic, and such cases do exist. But many, many more people have been traumatized who don't stand out in these exaggerated ways—even though they bear much in common with these cultural stereotypes.

Randy was a policeman. He worked in the inner city with a special unit that dealt with violent situations. He never fired his weapon, but he was often in confrontations with people who had weapons. He was stabbed and hurt physically several times; he saw a number of citizens hurt badly and was often exposed to the aftermath of violent death. Unlike many of his colleagues, however, Randy didn't resort to drinking or drugs—he kept all the tremendous stress of his work inside. His partner committed suicide, but Randy still showed no overt signs of problems. However, one day several months after his partner's death, as Randy got ready to go to work, he put his uniform on, started shaking, and couldn't stop. In fact, over the next several weeks, Randy discovered that he couldn't even put on his uniform without getting the shakes.

Randy spent two more years trying to be a policeman. He was hospitalized for various physical ailments, went through a number of treatments, and was given a variety of leaves and light-duty assignments. But he never fully resumed his old job. His life fell apart; his marriage nearly failed, and he began to lose respect for himself. Randy was traumatized not by a single event, but by the gradual accumulation of stressful exposure to trauma.

Robert, the highly successful owner of an export business, lived in an expensive home filled with the objects of his greatest passion, art. One night, he awoke with the house in flames. He escaped unharmed, but his home was totally destroyed. His insurance wasn't adequate to replace even a tenth of the priceless art he had lost. Robert had never lived in fear—he had always had that basic feeling of security that most of us carry through our daily lives. But ever since the fire, his life hasn't been the same, and he feels as though it never will be. Each day has become difficult, something to be gotten through, not to anticipate with excitement, the way it used to be.

Robert no longer feels remotely secure. In fact, he is all too aware of how vulnerable he is, and how vulnerable everything he has is. Robert has been traumatized. His art was the greatest source of pleasure in his life, but now he is reluctant to acquire more of it. He is too aware of the ease with which it can be taken from him.

Cynthia grew up in a dysfunctional family. Her father drank and became very moralistic and demanding when he was drunk. Over several years, he came into her room at night and molested her. Cynthia tried to tell her mother, but her mother discouraged her and said that Cynthia was exaggerating. So Cynthia learned to keep it to herself.

Cynthia's molestation went on for about four years, until she was eight. But for years after that, she continued to live in fear of her father coming into her room at night. She often dreamed that it was still happening. Eventually, the nightmares died down, and Cynthia became involved in school activities. She was popular in high school, although she didn't date much. She got married before she finished college and had a daughter of her own when she was twenty-six.

Around that time, her world began to fall apart. It became nearly impossible for her to have sex with her husband. In fact, getting physically close to him at all was disturbing to her. She found herself fearful and distrustful of him, even though there was no rational reason for her to feel that way. She found herself thinking more about her father and how he had abused her and ignored her feelings. In fits of rage that she directed at her husband, comparisons with her father would come up. And she began to have nightmares again, mostly of men chasing her and threatening her. Her sleep deteriorated and she looked haggard. She became depressed.

Cynthia had escaped the effects of her trauma for years until the intimacy of family life brought back her feelings of being exploited and abused in a close relationship.

William, Lynn, Randy, Robert, and Cynthia have all been traumatized. What happened to each of them and what it means is different, yet they have many things in common. Each felt that his or her life had been turned upside-down by an unforgettable event or series of events. These experiences stirred up massive emotions in them and left them with a general feeling that they were different from other people and that their lives were not nearly as secure as they had once believed. Each now lives with a feeling of uncertainty about the future, no longer confident that more traumatic things are not about to happen.

Each has pulled back from an old life, feeling somehow that he or she no longer fits in. Old pleasures have lost their meaning. All have struggled with feelings of anxiety and depression, and with physical problems, such as the shakes, sleep disorders, and digestive problems. William and Randy left their former professions where they had experienced the trauma. But Lynn and Robert continue to try to live their former lives, and most of the people they know have not noticed that they've changed. Cynthia's husband is aware that something is wrong, but he has difficulty linking her suspiciousness and anger to the molestation she experienced as a child.

The traumas that these individuals experienced were quite different—a physical attack, extended exposure to violence and fear, the sudden loss of a home and possessions, an abusive relationship with a father—yet all of them reacted in similar ways. The similarity of their reactions is what marks them all as traumatized. The precipitating event—the trauma —may be more or less severe in the eyes of an outsider, but we can only determine whether a person is traumatized by their *reaction* to an event. We can safely say that the more traumatic an event appears to be, the greater the likelihood that the person will be traumatized by it. We also know that the more people are exposed to traumatic stresses, the greater the likelihood that they'll be traumatized. But the ultimate determination of whether a person has been traumatized lies in his or her reaction, not in the event itself.

Diagnosing Traumatization

Diagnostic labeling by mental health professionals is sometimes very rigid, and sometimes people whose symptoms do not warrant an official diagnosis may still require treatment. Professionals often have a sort of either/or thinking about certain psychological disorders: If an individual meets all the criteria, he has the disorder; if he doesn't meet all the criteria, then he doesn't have the disorder.

This either/or thinking applies to the diagnosis of traumatization, Post-traumatic Stress Disorder (PTSD). It was acknowledged and added to the official manual of psychiatric diagnoses, the American Psychiatric Association's *Diagnostic and Statistical Manual*, only in the late 1970s. The *DSM* provides a list of criteria that must be met in order to warrant the diagnosis of PTSD. This diagnosis inevitably points the finger of causality every time it is used. Consequently, it has been the subject of a certain amount of controversy and may already be more of an either/or–type diagnosis than we need. My feeling is that PTSD should not be viewed as an either/or phenomenon. I believe there is a continuum of traumatization; some people are mildly traumatized, while others are severely affected. You can't be a little bit pregnant, but you *can* be a little bit traumatized.

I am not the only mental health professional who feels this way. During the middle and late 1980s, one of the largest and most comprehensive research projects ever undertaken —the National Vietnam Veterans Readjustment Study—was performed to assess the extent of PTSD among Vietnam veterans. In order to go beyond the rigid criteria of the official *DSM* diagnosis, the study looked for "Partial PTSD" as well. This was the experimenters' way of assessing related traumatization problems that didn't meet the formal criteria of PTSD.

The Diagnosis of Post-traumatic Stress Disorder (PTSD)

The current formal criteria for a PTSD diagnosis require that the individual have been through some kind of event or events that lie "outside the range of usual human experience and that would be markedly distressing to almost anyone." The person must then experience the following symptoms for a period of at least a month:

A. He must continue to *reexperience* the trauma through at least one of the following: intrusive memories, dreams, flashbacks, or through becoming intensely distressed when encountering reminders, including symbolic ones, of the traumatic event.

B. He must persistently either (1) make *efforts to avoid* thoughts, feelings, or situational reminders associated with the trauma or (2) manifest a state of general *numbed responsiveness*. The numbing is reflected in things such as a loss of memory of important aspects of the trauma, loss of interest in activities once enjoyed, feelings of detachment from others, a restricted range of feelings, and a sense of a foreshortened future. The formal diagnosis requires a minimum of three separate symptoms.

C. He must show symptoms of a state of *heightened arousal* by having at least two of the following: sleep disorder, exaggerated startle response, a wary hypervigilant attitude, irritability or angry outbursts, difficulties with concentration, and physiological reactions to events that symbolize or resemble the traumatic event.

As you can see, someone who has everything except the proper minimum number of symptoms in one of the categories wouldn't qualify for an official diagnosis of PTSD. But it seems absurd to suggest that such a person hasn't been traumatized. There are other symptoms that frequently accompany the syndrome but that are not viewed as specific criteria for the diagnosis. These include depression, survivor guilt (which I will explain in Chapter 2), and drug and alcohol abuse.

The five individuals I cited before all qualify for the *DSM* diagnosis of PTSD. But the following description is of a woman who doesn't qualify for the formal diagnosis. Still, I view her as another person who has been traumatized.

Dale had been married for over twelve years when she unexpectedly got pregnant ten years ago. At that time, she and her husband, Ed, were ambivalent about having a child, especially considering her age, and she couldn't decide whether she should have an abortion or proceed with a high-risk pregnancy. As her pregnancy progressed, it was getting close to the point where abortion wouldn't have been allowed. Finally, they decided to have the abortion, and her husband took her to a clinic where they knew no one. Immediately afterward, they left on a vacation. It proved to be disastrous. Without being able to say exactly why, they hated the place, the food—everything they came in contact with.

The abortion seemed to become history, and their lives resumed. But in the years that ensued, they developed problems in their marriage. They found it increasingly difficult to maintain a sexual relationship. Nearly ten years after the abortion, during the course of their marital therapy with me, the incident came up once more. Dale and Ed had never openly discussed how they felt about their decision to abort Dale's pregnancy. But in therapy, their guilt, anger, and sadness were finally aired.

How someone responds to having an abortion depends upon the meaning of the experience to that individual. Those with strong convictions against abortion are certainly likely to be more upset and have more guilt. For Dale, it was very upsetting, and her symptoms resembled those of someone who had been traumatized. She didn't seem to reexperience the event, but she did become distressed on every anniversary of the trauma. She had no physical symptoms, but her memory of that period had definitely been impaired, and she had developed an amazing unconscious ability to avoid reminders of it.

As we discussed all this in therapy, it became evident that she had no recollection of significant portions of the experience. Indeed, it turned out that she had driven past the abortion clinic twice a day for ten years but never noticed it. When her husband told her where it was, she was completely surprised. And yet even after that realization, she *continued* to fail to notice it. It was clear to me that the abortion was a traumatic event for her, and that she remained affected in a variety of ways for many years afterward. The things I have to say about healing from a traumatization are quite applicable for Dale.

As you can see, "traumatic experiences" aren't limited to horrible car accidents, the death of a parent, or being mugged and raped. It isn't something that happens only to survivors of the Holocaust or to Vietnam veterans. Traumatization is defined by how upset and vulnerable an experience (or an accumulation of several experiences) has made a person feel, even if she "only" witnessed that horrible car accident or "only" went through a vicious divorce or the loss of a job, or a baby ten years ago. The first step in dealing with traumatization is to recognize the traumatic experiences in your life.

2

STILL STAGGERING FROM THE BLOW
Living with a Trauma

There's no single description for what life is like for all individuals with PTSD. Because of the many possible levels of traumatization, the symptoms vary considerably. For some, life becomes a boring, meaningless pursuit, with no emotional ups and downs, nothing to get excited about. For others, it is a perpetual struggle, and threats are everywhere. They are constantly uptight and on their guard, anticipating trouble at times when others would be relaxed. For still others, life becomes a big drag; they're depressed, and they slog through their days isolated from the rest of the world.

But despite all the differences, certain common themes weave through the experience of everyone who has a trauma disorder. If you or a loved one has been traumatized, you should be able to recognize these themes.

When a traumatization persists for more than a few weeks, it begins to become a whole way of life, and everything that matters to you is affected. It's not just the intrusive thoughts, it's the life you're leading as well, particularly the way you feel about yourself and where you belong in the world of people. The effects of the trauma itself—what I call the primary trauma—can be viewed separately from the changes in your relationships with other people (the secondary trauma). *Primary trauma* refers to the direct effects of the trauma on your thoughts and emotions—the reexperiencing, the emotional numbing, and the hyperarousal. *Secondary trauma* refers to the changes in your relationships and the way in which you view yourself, which is influenced by your relationships. This disruption of your social world is reflected in your symptoms of alienation and your difficulty with relationships. Let's look at one of the examples from Chapter 1 in order to get a feel for the basic difference between the symptoms of the primary and secondary traumas.

Randy, the policeman who was traumatized on his high-stress job, had both kinds of symptoms. The shakes and fearfulness he experienced when he put on his uniform were symptoms of the primary trauma; they were a direct physical reaction to the memory of his trauma and his fear of encountering similar events. But Randy also developed symptoms of secondary trauma. His friendships with other policemen declined, and he became isolated. He valued their friendship and saw his isolation as evidence that he was worthless. As his feelings about himself suffered, he became irritable and difficult to be around—which put considerable stress on his relationship with his wife.

Randy's shakes and anxiety were set off by a reminder of his primary trauma—his uniform. But his alienation, his lowered self-esteem, and his difficulty with intimacy were not directly related to his traumatic job. Rather, they reflected a breakdown in his relationships with other people and how he felt about himself. These symptoms were manifestations of his secondary trauma.

The Primary Trauma

The development of a trauma disorder begins with the experience of a trauma, whether it is a single event—such as an accident or natural disaster—or a series of highly stressful events, such as wartime duty or an abusive relationship. At the time of the event, you are so emotionally overwhelmed that you are unable to fully integrate your experience of it. At the time of the event, if you were to allow yourself to experience its full emotional impact, you'd be immobilized by the intensity of the emotions. And during a disaster, you cannot allow yourself to "fall apart"; you must control your feelings and maintain composure in order to take appropriate action. Similarly, you dare not give in to your feelings of outrage in an abusive relationship, or you could provoke further abuse. Even if there is no immediate, obvious danger, you tend to avoid letting yourself be overcome by extremely intense emotions. Consequently, you protect your functioning by shutting down your ability to have a spontaneous emotional reaction.

Overwhelming Emotion

Many people don't fully appreciate the notion of truly overwhelming emotion. But if I may offer a graphic example: Imagine a situation where you witness a human being being badly hurt or killed. Perhaps you see an auto accident, even live coverage of a catastrophe on television. Your feeling at this moment is overpowering; you may feel suddenly sick at your stomach. For an instant, you are under the sway of a traumatic emotion, the unthinkable anxiety that comes from helplessness in the face of something terrible happening to a human being. These emotions are overwhelming. Now imagine that you live with that overwhelming feeling just under the surface all the time. That is how it can feel to live with traumatization.

If you have undergone such a trauma, it's likely that you shut down significant parts of your spontaneous emotional reaction to the event, and perhaps even to the memory of it. You may have recalled the event as you were reading just now, started to feel that terrible feeling, and quickly shut down the overwhelming emotion so that the memory could be viewed dispassionately.

A couple of years ago, I witnessed a dog being hit by a high-speed car at a park. A number of bystanders saw the tragedy as well. I saw the dog run out in front of the car, and I was helpless to do anything to stop what I knew was about to happen. Afterward, all the bystanders were in a bit of a daze; everyone had stopped in their tracks and stood still for a moment, as if in shock. The memory of the impact came back to me several times over the next few days. This was an example of a traumatic emotion, the overwhelming helplessness and the horror that I and, I'm sure, many other people felt when that dog was hit.

Emotional Numbing

When you shut down your spontaneous emotional reaction because it is too overwhelming, part of your personality shuts down as well. You lose touch with the part of your own emotional makeup. You're able to function, but you're emotionally numb. And this numbness isn't restricted to the emotions surrounding trauma. It can become a way of life, a new part of your personality. This is particularly true if you've been repeatedly exposed to trauma. You quickly learn to numb out and insulate yourself from the effects of the continued exposure. Abused children grow up learning to numb out at a moment's notice, and by the time they're adults, emotional numbing is a way of life.

The price you pay for emotional numbing is to lose touch with the part of yourself that makes you feel alive inside. A deadness replaces the core of your emotional nature, and as this happens, you lose your ability to feel awe, wonder, and rapture. Many people who are emotionally numb pursue perilous life-styles to try to recapture those feelings. As one man described it, "I have such a jaded view of the world that nothing excites me or feels really important to me—the only thing that gets me up is living on the edge."

Emotional numbing is one of the most important survival mechanisms available to people who have been traumatized. Without it, they would quickly succumb to the overwhelming emotions. It's a critical adaptation to extreme circumstances. But it becomes maladaptive when it persists after the traumatic situation is over. And this is what happens when people develop PTSD. They continue to numb themselves, even though the threatening situation is over.

One of the things that I hear most consistently from Vietnam vets is that they developed an insensitivity to the horror and tragedy going on around them. They (and I) learned to numb out and pass through the experiences with deadened feelings, unaffected by things that would normally horrify them. For some, the numbing happened suddenly—in the aftermath of a particularly shattering traumatic experience. For others, it developed more slowly, often invisibly, until the realization of their deadened reactions dawned upon them. For many this emotional numbing was clearly a reaction to a specific trauma. But for others, it was an adaptation to living with the constant stress of life in Vietnam.

Virtually all the Vietnam veterans I've talked to describe this experience—not just the combat troops, but the nurses, administrative personnel, and others. There were many sources of extreme stress in Vietnam—combat is only the most obvious. One of the most stress-producing jobs was working with Graves Registration and dealing with the mangled bodies of the men killed in combat. This produced a very high number of traumatized individuals who never saw a shot fired.

Reexperiencing the Trauma

If you are a trauma survivor, the more you rely upon numbing to deaden potentially overwhelming emotions, the more you lose touch with your ability to spontaneously experience many kinds of emotion. It's important that you be able to experience a wide range of emotions—you need them in order to deal with life. Your emotions notify you when you should be careful in dangerous situations; they bond you to others and provide you with the motivation to strive in the face of adversity. You're handicapped without them. Other parts of your psychological makeup try to revive your ability to feel. In order to awaken those dormant aspects of your emotional life, your ego tries to reexpose you to your memories of the trauma. It does that by noticing every reminder and by thinking and dreaming about the trauma.

Your memories are more than just recollections of what has happened to you. They're composed of the intense sensations, thoughts, and feelings you experienced at the time of the event. When you live through a traumatic moment, you experience every nuance of that moment intensely. The sensory impressions associated with it are burned into your memory, as are the associated thoughts and feelings. In a sense, your ability to spontaneously experience your own emotions is locked away with your memories of the horrifying trauma. In order to unlock those spontaneous emotions, your ego must release those memories. But until they're released, your ability to spontaneously experience the full range of emotions will remain stunted. Yet unlocking your traumatic memories also restimulates the ego mechanisms that protected you from experiencing the overwhelming emotions in the first place—the mechanisms that shut down your emotions.

Paradoxically, your intrusive memories are an unconscious effort to break out of the emotional numbing, even though recalling those memories stimulates your ego to once more employ emotional numbing so that you won't be emotionally overwhelmed. You're caught in a vicious cycle—you dredge up emotionally loaded memories of your trauma, then shut yourself down again to avoid experiencing the overwhelming emotions. The result is that you periodically reexperience the trauma, then numb out again. This reexperiencing can take the form of flashbacks and dreams, as well as simply thinking about the trauma or being easily reminded of it.

Since the images recorded in your memory are linked to the sensory perceptions you experienced at the time of the trauma, each of your five senses—sight, hearing, smell, touch, taste—can participate in helping you recover a memory. You encounter a sensory reminder, and you suddenly recall the memory. Have you ever smelled a rose? How about vomit? (Sorry, I'm trying to make a point.) Did I get a reaction? Did you shudder, wrinkle your nose, or groan? If so, why do you think you reacted that way? You reacted not just to the word *vomit* but to all the sensory impressions you have tied up with that word—and I suggested you recall the smell. In just this way, traumatic memories are associated with sensory impressions.

Vietnam vets frequently react to the sound of helicopters, which they associate with Vietnam. They usually react to the helicopter sound by becoming vigilant. They scan the sky until they locate the source, and only then do they relax. Similarly, many women who were molested as children react to the weight of a man upon them during sex. Women who have been molested often feel claustrophobic and panicked, compelled to remove the person's weight and feel unrestrained before they can relax. For each, recalling buried memories brings back some of the associated emotions.

Living with the Primary Trauma

Most traumatized people live lives that are deadened by emotional numbing and periodically disrupted by the intrusion of disturbing memories and emotions related to the primary trauma. They seldom feel good; they feel either numb or not so good. If you have intrusive memories and emotional numbing but they don't seriously interfere with your life, chances are that you keep your traumatic memories effectively bottled up or that you pursue a life-style that allows you to control your symptoms. Such life-styles can include being a hermit and withdrawing from society, relying on alcohol or drugs to remain numb, living a sensation-seeking life to overcome the deadness inside, or making a career out of reliving the trauma.

The sensation-seeker pursues high adventure or takes extreme risks and lives like a sort of adrenaline addict, always seeking excitement highs. The person who makes a career out of reliving the trauma usually works in an area that requires the same skills as those used to survive the primary trauma, such as the combat veteran who becomes a policeman, fireman, or emergency medical worker. Obviously, some of these life-styles are more adaptive than others. If you've been traumatized, such adaptations can make it easier to keep an emotional distance from your traumatic memories. You'll probably be more able to recall the memories while, at the same time, you keep them separate from the overwhelming emotions associated with them.

Does every trauma survivor get caught in this need to dredge up and then numb out memories? Not all of them— many people who experience trauma never get caught in this vicious cycle. But every trauma survivor can conceivably develop it, even after functioning well for many years. People who aren't plagued by intrusive reexperiencing of a trauma are those whose personalities are well suited for ignoring disturbing emotions while continuing to function well. But it is my opinion that no one locks up the emotions associated with an extreme traumatic experience without paying a price of at least some deadness inside. People who know such individuals intimately report that there's something amiss in them, but they've learned to leave the subject alone.

The Secondary Trauma

The secondary trauma doesn't occur until sometime after the traumatic event. If you've been traumatized, at some point you realize that things have changed between you and others—you're no longer the same person you were before, and you can't enjoy yourself with others in the same way. In effect, the trauma has come back and traumatized you a second time. You must contend not only with the terrible event that happened to you, but with the person you've become as a result of it. You no longer feel that you are like others, and you've lost something in your sense of being connected with people. Living with your traumatization takes on a whole new dimension of loneliness. It's like discovering that you are defective and no longer a full-fledged member of society.

Damaged Connection with Others

The concept that you are connected to other people may be harder to grasp than the concept of intrusive memories. Connectedness is a feeling that makes you comfortable with others, a sense of sharing something in common. You feel connected to people with whom you share membership in a group. This starts with your family and includes many other groups throughout your life: school, work, community, and country. This sense of belonging to a group allows you to open yourself up and be vulnerable with others.

In secondary trauma, your feeling of belonging to a group is affected in two ways. First, the symptoms of your primary trauma make you feel that you're different from others, and second, others react to you differently. In cases of severe traumatization, you feel that you belong to no groups whatsoever because there is *no one* to whom you feel connected. In less severe cases, you may feel you can relate to some restricted groups, such as your loved ones or your fellow survivors.

Your strongest connections (to spouse, family, and close friends) will be the last to go, but one thing is certain: the greater the degree of your secondary traumatization, the fewer groups you'll find to which you feel you really belong.

Damaged Sense of Self

The other negative consequence of the secondary trauma is that your sense of self is affected. You've changed; you feel different because you *are* different, and you can tell that others see you as different. You have three changes to deal with: your internal view of yourself, others' view of you, and your loosened connection with others. These three changes adversely affect your sense of self.

Sense of self is a psychological term that is used often but hard to define clearly. It's sometimes used like the word *identity* to mean who you are. I use it more to mean the core of your sense of being a person. Your sense of self includes your sense of who you are, as well as what kind of person you are and how worthwhile you are. Thus, you must have a basic sense of self in order to have an identity, a self-concept, and high self-esteem.

If you're not accustomed to concepts like identity and self-esteem, this notion of a sense of self may be a bit murky to you. Let's look at an example.

Lynn, the woman who was mugged in the large city, had functioned very well prior to her mugging. She maintained an active social life, a satisfying career, and numerous hobbies and interests. We could say that she knew who and what she was, and that she felt connected to a variety of people and groups of people. Basically, she had a satisfying life. But after her traumatization, things changed. Her view of herself changed—and she saw herself as much more vulnerable, not the strong person she used to be. She became more anxious, stayed at home more, and was much more timid about taking risks. She also believed that others saw her differently, because their interactions with her changed. But since Lynn hadn't told most people about her trauma, their changed behavior was not a result of viewing her as traumatized. Rather, they were responding to the changes in her own behavior. Lynn was living with considerable fear, which she tried to control by keeping it to herself. This combination of fear and self-control interfered with her connection to others, and she began to feel increasingly alienated.

As a result of this alienation, Lynn's core feeling about herself was affected. She lost much of her self-esteem and became plagued with doubts about who she really was. She was no longer able to enjoy the activities that had previously made her life meaningful. The meaning she lost was replaced by a preoccupation with simply getting through each day. We can use many different concepts and labels to describe what Lynn was experiencing; I prefer to say that her very sense of herself as a person was shaken.

If your sense of self has been damaged, your feeling of basic worth as a person, and your ability to soothe your own anxieties and maintain control of your emotions, may fluctuate. You may feel that you're on an emotional roller-coaster, where your moods are swept about by relatively minor events. Your basic sense of self may be so tenuous that it falters in the face of any indication that you are not living up to your own or others' expectations of you.

Most people who suffer from a damaged sense of self do so because of events that occurred during their formative years in early childhood. It is then that people generally develop the solid sense of self that underlies their self-esteem and emotional balance in later life. But some people who have a solid sense of self lose it as a result of traumatization. In either case, if your sense of self has been affected, you must develop ways to control your emotions and regain your self-esteem.

Coping with Secondary Trauma

One way trauma survivors control their unstable emotions is by using the emotional numbing that they used during the primary trauma. This emotionally nonreactive state becomes the status quo for many trauma survivors, who go through life shut down emotionally, never getting terribly happy or terribly sad. But most of us cannot maintain emotional numbness all the time; we find ourselves periodically overwhelmed by feelings that we can't control. This can lead to sudden states of rage, tantrums over our frustration and lack of control. For others, the lack of emotional control depresses them and makes them feel helpless, and they get even more down.

Some people avoid directly experiencing their emotions by developing physical problems that preoccupy and distract them. Their feelings about their physical problems are often some of the same feelings they have about their emotional trauma: They're depressed, anxious, or enraged by their physical problems, just as they are about their trauma. For example, Randy became preoccupied with his physical health and worried constantly about it. He was concerned that he might have some fatal illness and sought out many doctors. This was actually a displacement of his fear that he might die on his dangerous job. But focusing on physical problems allowed him to focus on physical cures; he could search for the doctor, the drug, or the right technique. He could maintain the illusion that his feelings could be instantly fixed if he could only find the right remedy.

As I have mentioned, another problem created by a damaged sense of self is difficulty in maintaining self-esteem. If you have an impaired ability to sustain self-esteem, you tend to find less and less lasting means of feeling all right. You may fill your life with work or other accomplishments to feel good about yourself. As long as you're producing, you can feel okay. Or you may surround yourself with people who make you feel better about yourself, whether they are admirers or people toward whom you feel superior. You may be unable to acknowledge your shortcomings and become adept at blaming others. Or you may just accept a woeful view of yourself—a loser image.

All these styles of dealing with flagging self-esteem are available to trauma survivors. Some, to be sure, are less available than others. Because of their feelings of unconnectedness, for example, few trauma survivors are able to maintain relationships with admirers. It's also more difficult to fill their lives with accomplishments because of the other ways in which their functioning is impaired. Consequently, they tend to immerse themselves in work that doesn't involve too much contact with people, and/or they develop a style of always blaming others for problems, and/or they become increasingly depressed and dysfunctional.

Further Effects of Traumatization

If you have suffered a primary trauma, internally you're struggling with several problems: your vulnerability to being overwhelmed by emotions, the protective deadening you use to deal with them, and internal pressure to revive the traumatic memories in order to recover the ability to safely and spontaneously feel emotions. And if you have a secondary trauma, you're experiencing a loss of many of your good feelings about yourself, having feelings of alienation and detachment from others, and having difficulty in relationships. These are the central effects of traumatization—but unfortunately, they aren't the whole story.

Damaged Worldview

Traumatization also changes the way you see the world, including your view of yourself and your place in that world. Your worldview is composed of all the attitudes, preconceptions, ideas, and knowledge you have. In many respects, your worldview actually defines your perceptions. In the phenomenon known as *selective perception*, different people focus on different aspects of the same event. A policeman and a clothing designer see entirely different things when they survey a crowd of people. The policeman focuses on people's behavior, while the designer focuses on people's appearance. So their experiences (and recollections) of the same event are quite different. They are selectively perceiving that part of the event to which they are most attuned.

Selective perception suggests that your biases and attitudes also shape your perceptions. If you feel that people can't be trusted, then you notice every minor indicator that people are not behaving in trustworthy ways. When you read the newspaper, you catch every headline that confirms your view, but you do not focus on headlines that might represent a more optimistic view.

When you're traumatized, you're more attuned to dangers than you used to be. It feels as if you have become a different person living in a different world. When your worldview changes, in a very real sense, your whole world changes.

Loss of Illusions of Security

One aspect of your altered worldview is the loss of your illusions of security. You're suddenly aware of your vulnerability to dangers that you had previously ignored. If you haven't been traumatized, you may not realize how much you maintain illusions of security. But consider: You drive a vehicle that weighs several thousand pounds, and its mechanical reliability and your consequent safety are often in the hands of people you don't even know. You pilot it along busy roads among thousands of other equally heavy or even heavier vehicles, driven by a mass of humanity who have widely different levels of driving skill and motivations to drive carefully. Approximately fifty thousand people die on U.S. highways each year. An enormous number of drivers are legally drunk while driving, particularly on Saturday nights. And the majority of accidents occur within twenty-five miles of home. You know what happens to human beings in bad auto accidents—they're so common that you have probably seen accidents or their aftermath personally. Yet every day, you blithely get into your car and zip off to the grocery store under the illusion that you're as safe as if you were sitting on the sofa. Your illusions of security allow you to cope with many of the common dangers of everyday life without becoming preoccupied with them.

If you've been traumatized, however, you have a different view of the world and its dangers. You find it difficult to maintain illusions of security because you know what could potentially happen. You're no longer able to maintain the belief that accidents, illnesses, and bad things only happen to the "other guy" and never to you. We've all had our illusions of security dim at times—we usually drive a little more safely after viewing an accident. But when you've been traumatized, the dimming of those illusions is no longer just temporary. Often, illusions of security are lost altogether.

Loss of Meaning

Each of us needs to find some meaning in our existence, and we do it in many different ways. People find meaning through religion, family, work, or even play. Some people find it by helping their fellow man; others find it by providing the most enjoyment for themselves. But somehow, everyone finds some reason to want to live and to want to live in a certain way.

The meanings we find change as our lives change, but usually those changes are gradual. There are occasional sudden shifts when we make transitions through life stages, such as marriage and parenthood. For those changes, social institutions—such as ceremonies and well-defined roles—help us make the adjustments. But traumatization causes a sudden wrenching of our personal meanings for our lives. And unfortunately, fewer social institutions tend to be available to help us negotiate that kind of change.

If your life loses meaning, you're thrown into a state of uncertainty. You're no longer sure what's important to you, and this uncertainty interferes with your ability to pursue your goals. It is difficult enough to attain a long-term goal, such as getting a higher education or maintaining a lifelong relationship. The secret to attaining such goals is to tolerate the short-term frustrations by keeping sight of the long-term payoff. But if the meaning in your life is lost, you may not be so sure that there *is* any long-term payoff. And when you lose that certainty, the short-term frustrations become too much for you to bear. So you give up on your goal—be it a relationship, a project, a job, or a self-improvement program.

When Elizabeth was a nurse in Vietnam, she was exposed to tremendous amounts of trauma. She worked with men who were horribly maimed and saw hundreds of her patients die. But she felt that what she was doing was immensely important, worthwhile, and meaningful, so she was able to tolerate the daily stress. After she returned home from the war, she continued to pursue a meaningful life by teaching others and passing on some of the valuable knowledge she'd acquired. But then a close friend, another nurse from Vietnam, committed suicide. Suddenly, Elizabeth felt useless, that her life was meaningless, hollow. She felt she was not doing anything that justified her existence—and she responded to this by giving up her career.

The suicide of Elizabeth's friend made her question almost everything she'd ever considered worth living for, and she "just curled up emotionally and withdrew." She went from finding considerable meaning in her life to questioning whether life was even worth living. Elizabeth's story is a dramatic example of someone whose life loses meaning as a result of traumatization. It also illustrates how finding meaning in work allows a person to tolerate incredible levels of stress. She had successfully coped with daily exposure to powerful trauma for many years.

Loss of Feeling of Control

Some people feel that they're in control of their lives. They live where they live and do what they do because they've chosen to do these things. Such people are said to have an *internal locus of control*. They regard the basic control over their lives as existing *within* themselves. Other people have an *external locus of control*. They don't feel that they have much control over their own lives. They believe that what happens to them is mostly the result of external events. All they can do is go along with things, making the best of it all. People who see themselves as having very little control over their lives are vulnerable to depression if things go badly because they feel powerless to do anything about it.

Traumatization can damage your feeling that you're in control of your own life. Someone with an internal locus of control suddenly has an external one. You can develop a sort of victim identity, in which you always see yourself as a victim, the pawn of external events. Under such circumstances, you may reason, why strive for more, why try to make things better? It's all beyond your control anyway.

Clearly, this is a destructive attitude. In his book *Man's Search for Meaning*, Victor Frankl described his experience in the Nazi concentration camps. He noted that some prisoners just gave up, and he could tell that they were going to die. He realized that the Nazis could control all the external events, but he still had control over his attitude. Having this one piece of control gave him the strength to maintain hope, to find meaning, and to keep sight of the long-term payoff of surviving. He recognized the importance of finding the meaning in life, and because of it he was able to tolerate an enormously stressful experience.

Avoidance

Avoiding Traumatic Reminders

If you're besieged by intrusive memories, you live in fear of being reminded of your trauma. All kinds of things can serve as reminders, not only tangibles like Randy's uniform but intangibles like situations and relationships. In fact, it seems that for a lot of trauma survivors their strongest feelings rise to the surface when they experience the intensity of a very close relationship. This intensity connects them with the strong feelings associated with the trauma.

Some people are so sensitive to stimuli that remind them of their trauma that they must retreat from *all* relationships and activity that involves other people in order to avoid them. But what you avoid depends upon the stimuli to which you are most vulnerable. A jungle combat vet might steer clear of thickly foliated countryside, while a crime victim may avoid the urban jungle.

Lynn's mugging took place in a parking lot in a large city. It was dark but not terribly late, and there were other people around, but no one was close by at the moment of the attack. Lynn subsequently became sensitive to a number of reminders of her attack. She became very fearful about going out after dark, and she viewed parking lots as particularly dangerous. She learned to alter her shopping routines so as to not be in a parking lot after dark. She became highly attuned to the other people who were on the street when she was out. She learned to wait for a man to leave her office building so that she wouldn't have to walk to her car alone.

Clearly, many of Lynn's actions are realistic precautions that anyone would take to avoid a mugging. But she was also avoiding the anxiety that accompanied the memories of her attack. She became afraid of the dark because she knew what kind of terrors can be encountered in the dark. She was not really much safer in the daytime—it was simply that her attack took place in the dark. So in addition to the realistic possibility of another attack, darkness is linked to her feelings of helplessness and terror from the first attack.

Avoidance as a Life-style

You may not realize how much your life has come to center on avoiding reminders of your trauma. You may be steering clear of reminders automatically, without thinking; you may believe that you've chosen to live the way you do for reasons that have nothing to do with your traumatization. You rationalize your behavior in order to explain it to yourself and others. For example, a woman who has been raped and proceeds to find something wrong with every man she goes out with may be looking for a way of explaining why she can't let herself get close with a man. She rationalizes that something is wrong with this one, and something else is wrong with that one. But she ignores the fact that the very prospect of getting involved with a man stirs up her fearful feelings from the rape. She doesn't trust any man but instead of focusing on that, she focuses on the superficial shortcomings of each one she comes across.

The longer your traumatization goes unresolved, the

more your entire life-style becomes devoted to avoiding re-minders of it. At first, you may be aware of the reason that you get anxious around certain situations, and you actively avoid them. But the longer it goes on, the more you forget why the situation must be avoided, and you do it automati-cally. Certainly, many situations will always be directly linked to the trauma, and you know full well why you stay away from those situations. But there are many, many more situations in which the link to the trauma is less obvious, yet you learn to stay away from those as well.

Elizabeth left the field of nursing after her friend's death opened up her feelings about the trauma she had experi-enced in Vietnam. She says she just "lost interest in nursing" and told herself that training others and performing rela-tively mild nursing work in the States was just not as fulfill-ing as her work in the war. Years after she left nursing, her husband underwent surgery, and she was exposed to the sights, sounds, smells, and caretaking situations of nursing once more. She reacted to these reminders of her trauma by becoming very uncomfortable. The experience of dealing with her husband's surgery brought back many of the memo-ries and feelings that she had had in Vietnam. And she found herself avoiding the hospital and becoming numb again when she had to deal with her husband's physical needs.

Elizabeth had believed her decision to leave nursing was unrelated to her traumatization. But twenty years after her trauma, nursing still brought back traumatic memories. Therefore, her decision to leave her profession was surely influenced by its power to remind her of her traumatization.

Hyperarousal

Sleep Problems

Living in a state of heightened arousal from traumatiza-tion means you go through life with your motor running all the time. This ongoing state of arousal is reflected in a num-ber of different symptoms, the most common of which are sleep problems. You have trouble turning off long enough to fall asleep, or you wake easily at night and have difficulty falling back asleep.

When hyperarousal severely interferes with sleeping, a common "solution" is to develop an appetite for alcohol. But people who drink to sleep tend to wake up early because the effect of the alcohol begins to wear off. (Sometimes the early wakening is mistakenly seen as caused by depression.) Such people habitually fail to get enough sleep, which contributes to their lowered stress tolerance and ongoing state of fatigue. And, of course, their dependence upon alcohol leads to further problems with their health, relationships, and self-esteem.

Another way some people cope with sleep problems is to work themselves into a state of exhaustion. They work at multiple jobs or pursue leisure activities at a pace that is totally exhausting. This enables them to literally "fall into bed" at the end of the day and fall asleep. One Vietnam veteran who lived this way commented, "I'm never really relaxed until I've exhausted every muscle in my body. I feel best when I burn all over."

Other people pursue such "solutions" in order to avoid dreaming about the trauma. Neither the drinker nor the physically exhausted person recalls his dreams because he's too "out of it" when he sleeps. Some people are so upset by their trauma dreams that they exhaust themselves in order to be in a state where it's nearly impossible to dream. If you have trauma dreams, you know they can be as bad as the trauma itself. In your dreams, you're vulnerable to all the overwhelming feelings that you suppressed at the time of the trauma.

Startle Response

The state of heightened arousal can also produce exaggerated startle response, which means that you're very touchy and easily startled. This is the scientific term for the old cliché from movies where the combat veteran dives for cover when he hears a car backfire or firecrackers go off. Obviously, the veteran's sensitivity to such noises is very adaptive when he is in combat, but it is out of place back in the peaceful environment of his hometown. But exaggerated startle response is not confined to combat veterans. It is a characteristic of many kinds of traumatized people who have concluded that the world isn't safe. They are constantly prepared for further trauma and jump when they encounter anything that might represent danger.

The "Fight-or-Flight" Response

The "fight-or-flight" response is a physiological state that all animals enter when they perceive danger. Certain functions shut down, such as the flow of blood to the organs that are involved in digesting food, and other functions step up, such as the flow of blood to muscles. The glands that produce adrenaline go to work, and the nervous system makes major changes in preparation for action. It's similar to the battle station alarm sounded on a warship—everybody leaves the mess hall and goes to the spot where they'll be most useful if there's a battle. In a sense, this is also what happens with many trauma survivors. They are constantly at their battle stations and prepared to fight or flee.

This state of hyperpreparedness takes a considerable toll on you. You're prone to become irritable and subject to angry outbursts. You're like a football lineman in the final seconds of a close game—it's easy to jump offside because you're so keyed up to react quickly. Indeed, a failure to react represents death in many traumatic situations. If you're taken off guard, you're likely to be traumatized again. So you stay prepared, and inevitably "jump offside" now and then.

There are other costs to maintaining a state of always being prepared for disaster—physical costs. The warship that stays at battle stations too long ends up with a bunch of hungry and fatigued men. Likewise, your body isn't built to stay in the fight-or-flight state for extended periods of time. You need to have your down time—opportunities to rest,

relax, and recharge your batteries. If you don't take these opportunities, you can overtax your body and pay a physical
price. Your immune system breaks down, and you catch a
virus. Your blood pressure builds, and you have a heart attack. Your stomach produces excess acids, and you develop
an ulcer. Your muscles remain tense too long, and you get
cramps, backaches, and headaches. Your inner harmony de-
teriorates, and you become nervous and fidgety, uncertain of
yourself.

You can't maintain a constant state of fight-or-flight
arousal—your body chemistry won't allow it. But you can
come close to it if you maintain the vigilant attitude and constant preparedness for danger. If you never feel that you're
safe, you're likely to carry excessive arousal with you even
into your sleep. Thus, developing mechanisms—such as hobbies—for relaxing and feeling safe are prime goals to overcoming excessive arousal.

Randy, the policeman who was traumatized by the
accumulation of stress on his job, was unable to relax. Early
in his career, he had been very active in sports, and he had
found this to be a tremendous outlet for the tensions he acquired on the job. But after his exposure to traumatic stress
had built to a certain pitch, he was unable to get the same
level of relief from sports. More than that, he developed a
number of physical problems. He worked harder than ever at
the sports, but he started developing more injuries. The injuries finally reached the point where he was unable to pursue
sports at all. Then other physical problems developed. He got
headaches and was sick more often. He developed anxiety
symptoms and had several panic attacks in which he went to
emergency rooms fearing that he was having a heart attack
(a common form of panic or anxiety attack). It wasn't until
several years after he'd left the job that his physical problems
subsided.

Other Physical Costs

Other physiological symptoms can result from a preoccupation with a physical problem that a traumatized person develops to divert attention from intrusive memories. This preoccupation becomes an intrusion into your normal life, much like the traumatic memories that the physical problem displaces. The feelings you have about your physical problem are also similar to the feelings you might have about your memories of the trauma, were you to remember it directly. In this case, however, you attribute your anxiety and preoccupation to your physical symptoms and thus see no connection between it and the primary trauma.

Bill, as a marine in Vietnam, spent virtually all his time on missions deep in enemy territory, commanding a small team of four or five men. Their job was to spy on and ambush the enemy. His unit's survival depended upon not being discovered because if they were, they were sure to be outnumbered and would have little chance of escape. As leader, Bill worried about his team's survival. During the forays into the jungle, he focused on the task at hand and did his job well. Even so, when he was in the rear area awaiting the next mission, he worried constantly about where his team would be sent next. Bill didn't share these fears with anyone, feeling it was important for him to appear calm in order to inspire his men with confidence. Bill successfully led his team on more than fifty missions and never lost a man. He returned home with only minor wounds.

He made the transition back into civilian life with little difficulty, finishing college and starting a successful career in business. For about fifteen years, he did not talk about his experience in Vietnam. His life went along just fine, and he had no reason to feel that he'd been traumatized.

Then he started to develop some minor physical symptoms—intestinal problems, pain and weakness. His symptoms were not severe, but they were cause for concern, and he was forced to give up his program of regular exercise. His physicians couldn't explain the cause of the symptoms, so they admitted him to the hospital to do extensive tests. They told him that they thought he had cancer, but after several weeks, they concluded that he didn't. Yet still they couldn't explain his symptoms. They told him to go home and not worry about it.

Needless to say, he continued to worry about it. In fact, Bill became obsessed with his physical problems. It was less the amount of pain or discomfort he experienced than the uncertainty about what the symptoms represented. His life appeared unchanged to his work associates, but inside he was distraught and constantly preoccupied with his "illness."

In my view, Bill was once again experiencing the traumatization of his wartime experience. The focus of his fear was the uncertainty, similar to the uncertainty he had felt every time he took his team into enemy territory, never knowing what they would encounter. His psychological anxiety was displaced into physical symptoms.

It would be difficult to give Bill the official diagnosis of PTSD because he didn't have the intrusive reexperiencing of Vietnam. Or did he? We usually think of the reexperiencing as dreams, flashbacks, or memories of the actual event. But Bill's traumatic stress was related less to a single incident of combat than to his reliving the fear, uncertainty, and constant threat of being discovered.

Such physiological reactions to stress can be immense. I've seen these reactions in many different forms among Vietnam veterans. The combat veterans who were in frequent battles had an outlet for their fear—they could shoot back. But the men and women who were exposed to the dangers of the war without the opportunity to shoot back had to find other outlets for their stress and fear. The less free they were to talk about those feelings, the more likely they were to develop physical problems such as ulcers, headaches, intestinal problems, irritable bowel syndrome, tachycardia, and other kinds of disorders. I'm not talking about hypochondriacs— people who play up their minor physical symptoms. I'm talking about real physical problems that develop as a result of living with stress and carrying great tensions without adequate outlets.

We see the result of normal stress all around us—the little aches and pains we all develop when life is too much for us. Think about the difference between normal stressful events—such as the pace of modern life—and traumatic events, and you begin to appreciate how deep the impact of traumatic stress can go.

Fatigue and Depression

The Fatigue of Stress

Living with an unrecovered case of traumatization is very fatiguing; it can seem as if everything you do requires so much effort. Since your psychological apparatus for dealing with stress is working overtime dealing with the traumatization, you have few reserves to deal with other stresses in your life. You can easily become fatigued, irritated, or withdrawn. But whether you react by getting angry or depressed or by becoming more emotionally numb, the daily stresses of life are harder to cope with than they were before your traumatization.

Your fatigue is worse if you're in the midst of struggling with intrusive memories; trying to control them drains your psychological apparatus for dealing with stress. And your fatigue can be disguised by the use of alcohol and other drugs, if you've turned to them for help. Of course, that "solution" always creates new problems. (In Chapter 9, we'll look at some better solutions for dealing with fatigue and stress.)

Depression

Many people who have been traumatized are depressed. They lose their zest for life and feel down all the time. Some of those people are misdiagnosed. Their depression is obvious, so it's easy to miss their traumatization because depression can mask many of its symptoms. Depression is a natural reaction to traumatization, though not all people react this way, and the two may or may not be related.

There is a diversity of professional opinion on the reasons for depression. Depression has traditionally been understood to be a reaction to disturbing life events, usually ones involving loss. But in recent years, research has shown that many depressed people have a chemical disorder that is probably inherited. The professionals who are most committed to this biological view of depression support the use of antidepressant medications in treating it. It's logical, they feel, to treat a chemical imbalance with chemicals. Other professionals object to the standard use of antidepressants, and some are opposed to *ever* using them, except in the most severe circumstances. What this can mean to you is that your treatment can vary radically depending upon the orientation of the professional you see. (We'll discuss the issue of selecting a professional and the best form of treatment in Chapter 12.) I would advise avoiding anyone who insists there's only one way to treat your depression, whether it's always with drugs or always without.

But for now let's look a little closer at the symptom of depression itself. Depression is a mood disorder. We all experience higher and lower moods, but depression is a low mood in which you feel the blues, blah, or downright rotten. It can interfere with your memory, your concentration, and your thinking processes. It can affect your physical functioning. Some people are mildly depressed and have no physical symptoms. But the more depressed you are, the more likely it is that you'll have physical symptoms, such as slower reflexes, lower energy level, a decreased sex drive, and sleeping problems. And of course, depression can affect your spirit: you can have more negative thoughts, be more pessimistic, and have lower self-esteem. Additionally, depressed patients consistently complain that other people are turned off by their depression and avoid them. Thus, being depressed can resemble the alienation of the secondary trauma and can magnify the secondary trauma.

Our understanding of depression has increased significantly in recent years. As a result, we now recognize a range of variations and types of depression. We've learned that many of the more clearly biological forms of depression are related to chemical changes in the body (such as a woman's menstrual cycle), the seasons of the year, or even the amount of sunlight to which a person is exposed. But we also recognize the power of nonbiological, psychological factors such as the quality of relationships or the anniversary of a significant loss. A reactive depression is one that seems to be clearly a *reaction* to an event in your life. The depression that accompanies a trauma disorder is obviously reactive, but this doesn't necessarily mean you don't have a biological depression as well.

Survivor Guilt

If you were traumatized at a time when you were alone, you probably don't have feelings about other people being hurt. But if the trauma occurred in some kind of group situation, you may have feelings about how you were affected in comparison to the other people involved. If others were injured or killed, you may feel guilty that you survived and they did not, or that they didn't fare as well as you did. We call this phenomenon *survivor guilt*.

Survivor guilt was presented very well in the movie *Ordinary People*, in which a teenager survives a boating accident in which his brother was killed. Afterward, he is very troubled, and in the course of his psychotherapy, he learns that it is because he feels guilty that he lived when his brother did not. If you live with this kind of guilt, you may not be aware of it, or you may be unaware of the degree to which it affects your daily life. You might be living in a fashion that serves as your punishment. You may pursue self-destructive behaviors such as drug abuse or fighting. Or you may deprive yourself of any pleasures in life, work excessively, refuse to buy yourself nice things, or not take proper care of yourself.

Survivor guilt is most clearly seen in situations where the survivor experienced the same trauma as the person who died. Thus, the survivor of an auto crash in which others were killed is obviously vulnerable to developing survivor guilt. But survivor guilt also occurs in situations where people were exposed to different traumatic events. One man who survived a car crash developed survivor guilt a year later, when a close friend was drowned in a rafting accident. He related the two events in his mind and felt guilty that he lived when his friend didn't. Survivor guilt has been reported by people who survived serious illnesses, then saw someone else succumb to one. These people develop the illogical notion that their own survival has been bought at the cost of another's loss.

Kirk went to Vietnam during the heavy fighting of 1968. He was a noncombatant with an administrative job that prevented him from ever getting close to the fighting. Nevertheless, he heard about the heavy casualties and felt some guilt that he had such a safe position. After his tour of duty, he returned home and left the service. A few weeks after his discharge, he ran into a high school acquaintance who was also recently home from Vietnam and who had been involved in heavy fighting. This man shared some of his experiences with Kirk, particularly the letdown of his return to the States. The man was depressed and clearly affected by his combat experience. Shortly after their conversation, the combat veteran committed suicide. Subsequently, Kirk turned into a workaholic who never found time for himself. He never spent money on himself and always put himself down when talking with others.

When Kirk entered psychotherapy, he became aware of how terribly guilty he felt. He believed he should have done something to prevent the man's suicide and that "it simply wasn't fair" that he himself had "sailed through his tour in Vietnam" while this other man was exposed to extreme trauma. Kirk had survivor guilt (and many other symptoms of PTSD), and he was traumatized by his friend's suicide.

There are many reasons why people respond to the misfortunes of others by feeling guilty. Although Kirk felt guilty that he'd avoided combat, he may have already had a tendency to feel guilty that he learned in childhood. Nor is survivor guilt limited to those who avoided a serious trauma that got someone else. Many people who have been badly injured in accidents still feel guilty because someone else was badly injured or killed. The fact that they paid an obvious physical price doesn't seem to prevent survivor guilt in them.

Survivor guilt is rampant among Vietnam veterans who were exposed to severe trauma. Men who survived lots of heavy combat often extended their time in the combat zone or returned for additional tours because they felt guilty for surviving. Because of the way the rotation system was set up, the experienced troops always left less-experienced men behind when their tours ended. It's common for combat veterans to feel guilty about going home and to worry about what happened to the less-experienced men after they left.

For most people who suffer from survivor guilt, the underlying issue is not simply that they survived but that they feel relief that they survived. Most people suffering from survivor guilt are not consciously aware of this relief. Irrationally, you may even feel that you are responsible, that you made some kind of bargain in which the other person was damaged or killed instead of you. You end up feeling a sense of responsibility for the other person's tragedy. It may sound illogical, but this kind of reasoning is often used when people try to make sense of surviving when someone else didn't. Many "deals" are made with God in situations where people fear for their life or the life of a loved one.

Feeling responsible for another's tragedy can be a way of avoiding the feelings of helplessness and lack of control that are part of the primary trauma. It's a way of hanging on to an internal locus of control, or even the illusion that you are invulnerable and can control traumatic events. You're so powerful that not only were you able to save yourself but you decided who to sacrifice in the process. As a result, although you feel guilty about your responsibility for letting something happen to someone else, you avoid feeling helpless.

Your guilt can also serve as an outlet for the outrage you feel at your helplessness and lack of control. Most of us can't stand feeling helpless and unable to control our world, so we get angry and blame ourselves for letting terrible things happen. Feeling anger is preferable to feeling that we really have no control over the terrible things in our lives. This side of survivor guilt is very visible among people who blame someone when something happens to a member of their family. The bearer of the bad news often encounters anger from family members, as if the family blames the messenger for the death.

When you have survivor guilt, you may also direct your feelings of anger and blame toward yourself. It's common for war veterans to be ambivalent about contacting the families of the friends they lost in the war. They say they don't want to upset the families and remind them of their loss. This is certainly a legitimate reason for ambivalence, but another reason is often the veteran's own survivor guilt. He blames himself for his companion's loss and anticipates that the family will blame him as well.

On the twentieth anniversary of the death of my best friend in Vietnam, I tracked down his parents and contacted them. I had thought about doing this many, many times before, but always found reasons to let it go. When I finally did it, I was very tentative. I didn't want to force them to talk about their loss if they didn't wish to revisit it. But I thought they might want to talk to me, as I wanted to talk to them. When I called them, they were receptive. But making that phone call was one of the hardest things I've ever done. It was a healing experience for me, and I think it helped some with my survivor guilt.

Survivor guilt is prevalent among the children of trauma survivors, who often feel that they're somehow part of that "deal" that their parents made with God. Children often feel that they are to be the reward for which the parent survived. Such children can feel a tremendous sense of responsibility. In a sense, it's as if they inherit their parent's survivor guilt.

3

STAGGERING IN SYNC
Loving a Trauma Survivor

Now you have an idea of how far-reaching the effects of traumatization can be on a trauma survivor. His or her life can literally be torn apart. But the effects of traumatization do not stop with the trauma survivor. The survivor's loved ones, those who are emotionally close to her, can also pay a mental, emotional, or even physical price. The effects of traumatization are easily passed on from parent to child, from child to parent, from spouse to spouse, or even from friend to friend. An entire family can be affected by one member's traumatization.

Marsha and Philip were high school sweethearts. Philip was a star athlete, and Marsha was a star pupil. Soon after he finished high school, Philip went to Vietnam and served in heavy combat, including the very stressful siege of Khe Sanh. He was badly wounded, but he recovered and seemed to have put his traumatic war experiences behind him. Marsha and Philip were married shortly after he was discharged, and they launched into a relatively normal life together. They had two children and successful careers while remaining active in church and community affairs.

More than ten years after they married, Philip began having nightmares and flashbacks of Vietnam. As with many Vietnam veterans, the reason for the long delay in the appearance of his symptoms is not clear. But his symptoms increased, and he became withdrawn and irritable with Marsha and the children. He spent long hours sitting in front of the television, and he no longer coached his son's Little League team or worked for the church. After a number of counseling sessions with his pastor, he withdrew from that relationship as well. He started attending group therapy sessions at a Vet Center, beginning many years of treatment. Meanwhile, his son and daughter entered their teenage years without a father actively involved in their lives.

The emergence of Philip's traumatization had a severe impact upon his life. He went from being a highly respected husband, father, and community member to being a neglectful husband and father who was very much at odds with his community. The neglect certainly had an effect upon his family, but the impact on the family was even broader than that. It's much easier to live with a husband and father who has never been involved than to lose one who was once heavily involved. The symptoms of Philip's traumatization affected his entire family.

In the early phases of the development of Philip's PTSD, everyone was supportive of him. The church came to his aid by providing emotional support and financial assistance and by helping him find jobs. Marsha was very understanding and worked extra hours when Philip became unable to hold a job. The children learned to be more patient with him, and the entire house became quieter as the family adjusted to Philip's irritable moods and disquieting flashbacks.

But as time passed and Philip didn't return to his old self, the support began to be strained. Philip steadily drained the resources of his church; he kept losing the jobs they helped him find and eventually soured the pastor on the usefulness of the counseling sessions. At home, the family established new living patterns that simply didn't include Dad. Philip continued to live in the family home (usually sitting in front of the TV), but in many respects, he no longer seemed a member of the family.

Marsha went through a period of fighting with Philip before she basically gave up and simply tolerated him. She was working more, and she had to compensate for Philip's absence in all the activities in which the children were involved. Consequently, her social life declined to the point where she lost almost all contact with her friends. Her own activities with the church declined, and she found that even when she had a rare opportunity to do some of the work she used to love to perform for the church, she really couldn't enjoy herself. She became depressed and very lonely.

Their oldest child, Gary, was eight when his father's PTSD first appeared. At first, Gary stuck up for his father whenever anyone was critical of him. Gary and Philip had been very close, particularly sharing athletic interests. Gary tried to help out more around the home, and he would defend his father when his parents argued. Then he went through a period of becoming obsessed with war. He bought toy weapons, read war comic books, and played war all the time. When he entered his teenage years, he became highly involved in dirt biking. He continued to play baseball, but he fell from the varsity to a second-string player and his interest in it declined. His father never came to his games anymore.

Gary spent his free time riding dirt bikes and was seldom at home. He continued to help his mother quite a bit, and he maintained good grades in school. But he stopped taking his father's side. Instead, he became critical of him, and Marsha began to defend Philip to Gary. Gary was very scornful whenever he spoke to his father, but Philip never confronted him about it, which only contributed to Gary's loss of respect for his father. Gary never seemed to have a good time anymore; he was angry at his father and always serious. He tried to take over many adult responsibilities around the home, such as discussing the family finances with his mother. She resisted letting Gary become too responsible for adult concerns, but she admitted that she was tempted because she felt so alone in dealing with it all.

Gary's younger sister, Suzanne, who was six when it began, reacted to the situation very differently. She'd always been fairly quiet, and now she became even quieter. She never took sides during arguments and seemed unaffected by the problems in her family, maintaining her few close friendships and continuing to do all the same things she'd always done. In fact, she acted as if she were completely oblivious to the situation. But over the years, her mother perceived that Suzanne was suffering silently. Suzanne never complained, but when pressed to discuss the situation at home, she would quietly cry, never able to say much about why.

This family was struggling with an unusually severe case of traumatization. Their reactions may be more extreme than most, but in many respects they're fairly typical. This family exemplifies many of the common dynamics we see among families of trauma survivors: There were major shifts in their relationships, with the son taking on some of the father's role and the father giving up most of his authority, the general level of family closeness declining and family members ending up feeling isolated from one another; the intimacy in the marriage was lost. Marsha felt guilty about getting fed up with her husband's symptoms and losing patience with him. Gary became preoccupied with his father's trauma and tried to relive it. And Suzanne became withdrawn and was emotionally numb much of the time, just like her father.

In effect, the family members began to show symptoms of traumatic stress—the reliving and preoccupation with the trauma—as well as the guilt, anger, depression, isolation, and emotional numbing. A close, supportive family became a fragmented group in which it was very difficult for members to share their feelings with one another.

In this chapter, we'll look more closely at the impact that a family member's traumatization has on the family, as well as at the effect that loved ones can have on the trauma survivor.

The Impact on the Loved Ones

One of the central messages of this book is that trauma affects entire families, even if only one individual was initially traumatized. If more than one family member was initially traumatized, it's easy to see how the entire family is affected. Families who are traumatized together, such as survivors of natural disasters, tend to deal with their traumatization together. It's no surprise that the members should all develop similar symptoms. But it often comes as a surprise that the same thing can occur in families where only one member has been traumatized. This section and the next show how other family members are affected and how the family relationships change as a result of one member's traumatization.

Reactions to a Family Member's Traumatization

You hear about trauma every day—the news is full of trauma—but you tend to be unaffected by it until it hits close to home. When you personally *relate* to something traumatic happening to someone, you react very differently. If the trauma you hear about is one that you've experienced yourself, you're more likely to relate to it intensely.

You can also personally relate to someone else's trauma if you feel related or connected to the person to whom it happened. We tend to feel more involved with someone whose house burns down in our neighborhood—even if we have never met them—than with someone whose house burns down across the nation. If you *witness* a trauma occurring to someone else, it's likely that you'll feel related and thus be affected. To some degree, you're likely to feel as though the trauma has happened to *you*. At the park, when I saw the dog being hit by a car and the owner suddenly struck with grief, I felt an empathic pang of loss, as though I'd lost my own dog. I related because I was a nearby witness and because I'm a dog owner and could imagine my dog getting hurt.

Certainly, you'll feel most personally related to a trauma victim when you are, in fact, related. If you love the person who was traumatized—as a friend or as a romantic partner —you'll feel, to some degree, that you've been traumatized yourself. Simply witnessing a trauma can traumatize the witness, even if you don't know the victim. So consider the implications if the trauma occurs to someone you love, and if you actually witness the event. It would be as if it had happened to you. And if you feel either personally responsible for the victim, as a parent feels, or excessively dependent upon the victim, as a child feels, then your own traumatization may even be *worse* than the victim's.

So you see that, to a greater or lesser extent, you can be traumatized yourself by what's happened to your loved one. You experience many of the same feelings as she does because you can't help but put yourself into her shoes. You may even feel the added burden of responsibility for what happened to her. Then the aftermath of the trauma comes. And you relate not only to what happened to her, but to what continues to happen—because it's happening to you as well.

Enduring the Survivor's Symptoms

Living with someone who has the symptoms of PTSD isn't easy. You are affected on a variety of levels. Concretely, if your intimate partner has a sleep disorder, your own sleep is affected. And on a feeling level, if your partner is withdrawn, irritable, and frequently reexperiencing a trauma, you're likely to feel rejected, abused, and frustrated at your inability to help.

People who are depressed invariably report that their depression has negative effects on others and that others come to avoid them and relate to them in only superficial terms. If you're trying to maintain a close relationship with someone who's depressed, your efforts to cheer him up generally fail. Over a period of time, you may stop asking how he is because the answer is always the same. You feel worse because you can't change how he's feeling, and he may begin to feel that you don't care since you've stopped asking. You can't win either way.

If your loved one has severe symptoms of emotional numbing, this also has a disconcerting effect upon you. You often can't tell whether he's numbed out or if he's become too jaded and cynical to really care anymore. Many people who rely on emotional numbing seem to be feeling things quite normally until the intensity increases or they have an experience that makes them feel particularly vulnerable. Then suddenly the feeling turns off. The effect on you can be devastating. You're feeling close and comfortable with your loved one, then all of a sudden you're a million miles apart. You may feel that you've suddenly become the enemy. Apparently, your loved one's empathy for you disappears. This is very hard to endure, especially when your loved one switches unpredictably from Dr. Jekyll to Mr. Hyde. You find yourself always preparing for this to happen, so you end up holding back yourself. Your loved one senses this, of course, and that adds to the tension between you.

Often, this unpredictable switching-off of empathy is accompanied by rage attacks. Your loved one can abruptly change from treating you as a support to behaving as though you're the source of all his problems. This has a devastating effect on your ability to remain close and supportive. You can easily respond in ways that confirm his fears: that he really doesn't matter to you, that you feel he's only a burden, that you don't understand, that you think he could control his symptoms if he'd only try, or that you think he's just feeling sorry for himself. We all tend to become defensive when we're attacked, and we often counterattack when we can. Some people believe that anger makes the truth come out. I disagree. I think we find things to say that will hurt, whether they're truthful or not.

The rage attacks are related to your traumatized loved one's state of hyperarousal. She hasn't relaxed; she's anticipating a recurrence around the next corner. She doesn't sleep well; she's irritable, jittery, distrustful, and startles at the least sound. The woman who was raped views every dark corner as a potential point of attack. The child who awoke in a fire dares not go to sleep. The man who survived an auto accident starts driving as if every other driver were about to lose control.

Being around such people is exhausting. It's an assault on your own illusions of security—maybe you're not really as safe as you thought. And it's wearing—the fact that she never relaxes makes it hard for you to relax. You become frustrated trying to reassure her that everything is okay. And as you become frustrated and exhausted, you become less effective in reassuring her. Trying to calm an anxious child is doomed to failure if you're not calm yourself. The child senses your anxiety and impatience and responds to that rather than to anything you say. The result is that you may actually stimulate further anxiety in the loved one because she is frightened that something else is disturbing you.

Problem Drinking

For many loved ones of trauma survivors, the symptom that most dominates their lives is the loved one's drinking. Much has been written about alcoholism and its effects upon family life. I doubt I'd be saying anything you didn't know if I enumerated the negative effects of alcoholism. Instead, I'd like to remind you of the diverse ways people manifest drinking problems, and how traumatization can be involved.

Many people view drinking problems in rigid stereotypes. They have images of the skid row bum or the person who starts drinking early in the morning. Such stereotypes make it easier for people with drinking problems—or family members—to deny them. The truth is that there are many different forms of problem drinking. Some problem drinkers do drink all day, while others drink only in the evenings, on weekends, or even less often. Some problem drinkers stay sober for weeks or months, then go on binges, while others get drunk every weekend. Many never get drunk but regularly consume large amounts of alcohol. A drinking problem isn't defined by the amount of alcohol consumed—it's defined by the problems the drinking creates in a person's life. If your loved one's drinking has led to poor work performance, health problems, dangerous behavior (like driving drunk), fighting with you, or other problems, then he has a drinking problem.

Many people turn to alcohol as a solution to some other problem, such as nervousness in social situations or difficulty falling asleep at night. People who've been traumatized may initially find that alcohol helps with their symptoms: it can help them get to sleep, temporarily reverse their depression, and contribute to their ability to numb their emotions. Other drugs can do these things, too, but alcohol seems to be the most popular. In either case, what at first seems to help soon becomes the biggest problem of all.

Some people are genetically more vulnerable than others to developing alcoholism. But people who've been traumatized are also more vulnerable to developing alcoholism because they're using it to deal with their symptoms, though they may not realize that that is what they're doing.

It's often you, the loved one, who finally brings the drinker's problem with alcohol to his attention. Many loved ones have been labeled *enablers* because they protect the drinker from the consequences of his drinking and thus enable him to continue his destructive pattern. Out of their desire to help, they keep picking him up when he falls rather than allowing him to suffer the consequences and thereby become motivated to do something about why he's falling in the first place. This means that you can be an important part of the problem, or an important part of the solution.

For some reason, we tend to look for someone to blame when there are alcohol problems. Perhaps because the act of drinking is a voluntary behavior, it's common to point the finger of blame at the drinker. Since no one likes to feel blamed for having problems, drinkers often resort to blam-

ing someone else, saying things like, "She drove me to it."
The spouses of problem drinkers frequently feel that it's indeed their fault; their spouse wouldn't be drinking if they
were better husbands and wives. But this guilty attitude only
hampers you. Blaming is destructive and interferes with being able to objectively address and solve the problem. Blaming is the first thing that must go.

If your loved one has a drinking or drugging problem,
you should seek help for both (or all) of you. High levels of
addiction need to be treated in intense treatment programs,
often requiring hospitalization. Less extreme forms of alcoholism are usually kept out of the hospital. But find a support
network, whether you go to a treatment program or use community support groups. Alcoholics Anonymous has helped
millions of men and women overcome alcoholism. Al-Anon
has helped millions of family members of alcoholics. Many
such organizations offer support to people with chemical dependency problems and to those of you who live with such
people. (See the appendix for more organizations and ad-
dresses.)

Transmission of Symptoms

One of the really curious aspects of traumatization is
that its symptoms are communicable. If you're intimately involved with someone who's been traumatized, you can literally pick up her symptoms. This may seem ludicrous, but
consider the effect of living in Marsha and Philip's family,
where Philip was emotionally numb practically all the time.
After a while, the entire family adapted to his withdrawal
and emotionlessness. Indeed, they often sat in the same room
and watched television with him, though he barely participated in any discussion. Marsha and the kids tolerated this
bizarre situation by relying upon the same mechanism as
Philip—emotional numbing. Though they attempted to carry
on normal conversation and activity around Philip, they
found that their normal conversation evolved into a flatter

tone—there were fewer highs and lows. They became less reactive to emotional events and more accustomed to an atmosphere that lacked liveliness.

It's no wonder that Marsha became depressed and that the children redirected their emotional lives outside their home, Suzanne through her friends and Gary with his dirt biking. Gary's adaptation to his emotionally dead home is typical of many trauma survivors. They find a job or a hobby that involves danger and excitement, seeking to overcome the emotional deadness inside through adrenaline highs.

Emotional numbing does not always mean a drab, depressing atmosphere. It also includes doing exciting things to overcome the emotional deadness. Some trauma survivors combat their emotional numbing by always being "on," the life of the party, if their personalities already lean in that direction. At first sight, you certainly wouldn't think that such people are emotionally numb, since emotionally numb people are usually fairly low key. But always being "on" can cover an impoverished ability to feel. The person who's always ready to "party" may be trying to compensate for what he doesn't feel inside by creating an image of how he'd like to feel on the outside.

So family members can pick up emotional numbing as a way of coping with the same disturbing symptom in their loved one. And once you're emotionally numb yourself, you're subject to feeling depressed just like your loved one and to resort to similar mechanisms to combat emotional numbing. These may include sensation-seeking life-styles or an addictive and excessive pursuit of eating, drinking, drugs, gambling, or sex.

Relating to the Traumatic Emotions

Your loved one's symptoms may also be transmitted to you through your experiencing the emotions associated with her primary trauma and your ability to *relate* to her trauma. Simply knowing that your loved one was raped, or burned, or lost all her possessions can be traumatizing to you. This phenomenon can deepen as you talk to her about her trauma. As she describes it and begins to relive it, you may vicariously live through it with her. If you're effectively empathizing with her as she talks about the trauma, you'll personally feel something of what she went through. You won't just have thoughts about it, you'll have an emotional reaction to it! You may not have the same feelings as she, but you'll have feelings of your own. You may not have a reaction strong enough to produce your own traumatization, but many people do.

A vivid example of traumatization-by-association is seen among female psychotherapists who've had intrusive memories and combat dreams after working with combat veteran patients. (I mention the gender of the therapists only to emphasize that they had never been near or shown much interest in combat.) Similar phenomena have been observed among male therapists working with female rape victims. Becoming intimately involved with another person's trauma can make it so real that it can become your own trauma as well. Thus, the full array of primary trauma symptoms can develop in intimate listeners. These include the reexperiencing, the heightened arousal symptoms, the emotional numbing, and all the mechanisms people employ to deal with these symptoms.

Shrinking Social World

Just as you can recreate the primary trauma, you can recreate the secondary trauma as well. This can occur in two ways. In the first, your preoccupation with your loved one's primary trauma and the traumatic emotions leads you to feel distant from others. In effect, you come to feel like a trauma survivor yourself—different, misunderstood, and not connected to the society around you.

The other way that you can acquire the secondary trauma is more troubling. Your other social relationships begin to break down because of your loyalty to the trauma survivor. When she withdraws, you're put in the position of choosing between keeping up your own outside relationships or staying home with her. If you go on with your own life, it widens the gap between you and her and contributes to the loss of her feeling of belonging to the intimate pairing formed by the two of you. This distance makes her feel resentful and more alienated, and it makes you feel guilty. But if you stay home with her, your own relationships are bound to suffer. In that case, she feels guilty and you feel resentful. Either way, there's conflict.

The Impact on the Family as a System

As we have seen, trauma has a very real effect on individual family members. But in addition to its effect on individual members, it affects the family on another level as well —the systemic level. That is, the trauma affects the family as a whole, or system. From the systemic point of view, we can discover underlying rules and patterns that govern the actions of every family member. This can give us more insight into why people behave as they do and what specifically needs to change in order to make things better.

Rules That Govern Family Relationships

All families have rules about the expression of emotion. Some families express powerful emotions like anger and grief loudly, with lots of gesturing and facial expression. They yell and scream and jump up and down. Other families express those same powerful emotions quietly, with very little gesturing or expression. Each of these family systems abides by underlying, unspoken (but well-understood) rules.

Family rules can govern how emotion is to be expressed, when it's to be expressed, whether it's to be expressed, and who can express it. Some family rules govern whether men can cry, whether children can express anger at their elders, or just how sad, angry, joyous, or affectionate family members are allowed to be. The rules may be different for subgroups (men may not be permitted to cry or be depressed, but women can) and for different individuals. Often, one member or subgroup of a family expresses emotions that other members experience but don't express (such as the mother who expresses everybody's sadness).

So in one family where there has been a traumatic loss, the mother may cry and express the sadness, the father may get angry, the daughter may get frightened, and the son may get depressed. Individually, their reactions are very different, but systemically they may represent the range of feelings that everyone is experiencing, and each member is expressing in his or her way according to the family's rules. These rules, however, can sometimes interfere with the process of recovery.

Stop and think about your own family. What rules govern the expression of emotion? How do those rules bear on you and your loved ones in dealing with trauma? Do they interfere with the effective expression of powerful emotions? If your family members are dealing with trauma, are they hampered by rules constraining them from being able to effectively deal with powerful emotional experiences?

- What recurring messages did you grow up with and do you still see being followed and passed on to younger generations?

- Do you have significant gaps in the emotions that are expressed in your family? Is it acceptable to be angry, sad, grief-stricken, or terribly fearful?

- Can people have conflicts and work them out? Are they eventually able to talk about their differences without getting overly defensive?

- Are family members able to be vulnerable and reveal their weaknesses, fears, and insecurities?

- Are people able to be affectionate with and supportive of each other?

- Is there a flexibility in the roles family members play? Can father and mother each be both a nurturing figure and a disciplinarian? In family conflicts, do people take different sides at different times, or does everyone always line up in the same coalitions?

- Does everyone in the family have a right to speak up with their feelings?

If so, identify the dysfunctional rules, talk about them with your loved ones, and change the rules to fit your family's needs. The more you can identify and talk about the rules that hold your family back, the less power those rules hold over you and the easier it'll be to change them.

Of course, some people can get past a loss without much grieving and can keep a trauma buried without it erupting into consciousness through intrusive memories. But in general, it's better to be able to express the powerful feelings associated with trauma and loss. The closer a family is, the better they usually are at expressing these feelings with one another.

The "Dry Drunk" Family

Considered as family systems, traumatized families have a lot in common with alcoholic families. They share a coping style—dealing with feelings through some mechanism other than open discussion. But the similarities between the traumatized family and the alcoholic family are clearest when alcohol is removed from the picture. Many alcoholics who give up alcohol continue to live according to the same old pattern; family members frequently say that the recovering alcoholic might just as well still be drinking, for all the difference it makes in their lives.

The pattern that continues is one in which the recovering alcoholic remains distant from those who matter to him and is unable to express important feelings. For example, the husband and father who was never around when he was drinking gives up alcohol but is still never around because of work or other commitments or new interests that absorb him. Stopping drinking makes profound changes in the life of an alcoholic, but it can have little effect in the most important relationships, where change requires more than the absence of alcohol.

Some people speak of alcoholics who've not given up the dysfunctional patterns that accompanied drinking as "dry drunks." The "dry drunk" family resembles many traumatized families in their difficulty experiencing and expressing powerful emotions. People in "dry drunk" families often "act out" powerful feelings rather than express them verbally. They usually have a lot of difficulty maintaining closeness, and spouses keep a constant distance by either fighting regularly or losing interest in each other. At some level, every member of such a family feels isolated. One of the primary benefits of close relationships—the feeling of not facing life alone—is often missing in these "dry drunk" families.

In both the "dry drunk" family and the traumatized family, the rules must change if the relationships are to improve. Here are some of the kinds of dysfunctional rules that we see in such families.

- Sadness is not to be expressed openly and directly, either by the whole family or by certain individuals or subgroups (males, females, children, parents).

- Fear and anger and affection are not to be acknowledged openly and directly.

- Conflict must be avoided at all costs.

- Vulnerability must be avoided at all costs (so everything can only be expressed through conflict).

- Forgiveness is a sign of weakness.
- No one is safe.
- No one is entirely trustworthy (even family members).
- People outside the family can't be trusted.
- Never give an inch.
- There is nothing worth getting upset over.

It's true that most children aren't told that excessive expression of sadness is not permitted, but many have been told to "stop that crying, or I'll give you something to cry about." Expressions like "If I ever spoke to my mother the way you're speaking to me" pass on family rules about the expression of emotion from generation to generation. Similarly, children acquire family attitudes about the ways other people express emotions. "No child of mine ever spoke like that" and "No daughter of mine would dress that way" are reactions to people outside the family that also define the acceptable range of emotional expression within the family.

Disowned Feelings

Many people who are in perpetual conflict are really struggling with what are called disowned feelings. Your loved one may have some bad feelings from her traumatization that she hasn't adequately sorted out. She feels bad, usually about herself, but she focuses on you as the source of these bad feelings. In effect, she disowns her bad feelings— "they're not mine, you put them there"—and blames you.

Not only do traumatized people sometimes blame their loved ones for their bad feelings, they may even provoke a loved one to play the appropriate role in the drama of "creating" the feelings. Both trauma survivors and family members know each other well enough to push each other's emotional "buttons" and stimulate feelings without even realizing that they are doing it. For example, if you have doubts about your-self, you can provoke your loved one to treat you as if he doesn't trust you. You might do this by keeping him in the dark about what you do with your time, even if you use your time innocently. When he gets emotional and harangues you about what he thinks you're doing, you can blame your doubts about yourself on him since you know you're inno-cent of any wrongdoing. Thus, you don't have to face the fact that the feelings started within yourself.

Trauma survivors disown their feelings for several rea-sons: They are dealing with powerful feelings, they are un-aware of the exact nature of their feelings, and they are operating according to rules they learned in childhood and that are still in force in the current family system. Violating the rules usually feels like an act of disloyalty, and many of the rules define the way a person is supposed to feel about him or herself. Thus, breaking them tends to be a blow to one's self-esteem. If a man is brought up to believe that it is unmanly to cry, he will likely disown feelings that might lead to tears and indeed feel he is being unmanly should he cry.

So as you can see, preexisting rules that interfere with the appropriate expression of powerful feelings can lead to excessive disowning of feelings and failure to be able to deal with severe emotional experiences like trauma. You take these rules with you through life; they become part of your personality—and they're hard to change. You may never no-tice that you are carrying many dysfunctional rules until you encounter a severe emotional event. But the rules are there, and they don't tend to change unless you make an effort to change them. You will recreate these internal rules in each "family" you become a part of throughout your life.

The Impact of Loved Ones on the Trauma Survivor

In the family situation we discussed at the beginning of this chapter, Philip's family reacted to the emergence of his traumatization initially by being supportive. Everyone understood that he was hurting inside and that it had to do with the terrible things he had experienced in the war. This is how most families respond to the traumatization of a family member. They care, and they want to help their wounded member recover from the trauma. But they don't always know how. Often their support fails to help, and they become frustrated and allow the loved one to withdraw into a shell. After a while, they may come to feel that the only thing they can do is to leave her alone and allow her to deal with it in her own way. But allowing any family member to become walled off from the rest produces an unhealthy atmosphere for everyone.

Avoidance

You may find yourself struggling with what to say and how to respond to a traumatized loved one. You have feelings about her, and you have your own emotional reactions to the trauma itself that you're not certain how to handle. But whether you realize it or not, you will be communicating these feelings unconsciously. Trauma survivors are particularly sensitive to communication that occurs through many channels, including tone of voice, eye contact, body language, choice of conversation topic, attitudes expressed about seemingly unrelated issues, and how much members make themselves available.

Although you say you want to hear all about the trauma, you may actually be conveying a totally different message in other ways. For instance, you may smile inappropriately when your loved one brings up the trauma, look away more than you normally do, or deny that the traumatization is upsetting—while your voice goes up an octave every time you speak about it. You may sit more stiffly or fidget with something or choose to sit in a chair that's too far away for intimate communication. You may leave the television on, hold the newspaper in your lap, or attempt to draw someone else into the conversation whenever the topic comes up.

Perhaps most significantly, you may selectively respond to what your loved one expresses—responding to the less disturbing aspects and ignoring the most upsetting parts. You likely are not doing this on purpose, and it doesn't necessarily mean that you don't want to listen and help. But your loved one may get the feeling that you're uncomfortable and don't really want to talk about it. She may fear that you find the emotions she's trying to control to be as overwhelming as she does, and that you don't want to encounter them either.

One family came for a counseling session after their college-age daughter Debbie was in a serious auto accident and started having nightmares. The family told her that they wanted to hear all about it, and so Debbie told the story of how she handled herself at the time of the wreck. She wasn't hurt and she performed admirably, helping the people in the other car and remaining very level-headed throughout. But the next day she had a case of the shakes and began to relive the accident in her mind. Then she became plagued with thoughts of the accident and couldn't sleep without dreaming about it.

Debbie's family seemed to listen attentively and communicated their concern and relief that she hadn't been injured. But they focused their comments on how well she'd handled the situation, and they kept reminding her that she'd come through it without injuries and now it was over with. Somehow Debbie felt dissatisfied with what they said, so she told them how scared she'd been. As they focused on the fearfulness of the event, she felt more understood and supported. She saw that they too had been scared, even after they'd learned she hadn't been hurt. She was then able to accept their helpful perspective that she had in fact survived. Her nightmares quickly dwindled away.

This family experienced a focused trauma that was briefly upsetting. It was all over in a couple of weeks because Debbie's family was very responsive to her and willing to do whatever was necessary to help. They had felt it would be more helpful to remind her of her strength because they thought she was too focused on her fearful feelings and they were trying to help her regain a balanced perspective. They thought that if they were to focus on how frightening the accident had been, they might confirm her fears and she might become permanently damaged. But to her, their failure to focus on her fearful feelings meant that they didn't really want to hear about them—despite what they claimed— and that they didn't trust that she could handle talking about them.

This example demonstrates how easily people can selectively respond to or steer away from the disturbing emotions associated with their loved one's trauma. You may feel it's better not to focus on the negative feelings, but you may also find them too disturbing yourself. Bear in mind that the reason the primary trauma keeps recurring is that the original emotions were so overwhelming that your loved one had to shut down her capacity to experience them. But now she needs to express her feelings to recover her ability to feel such things. In order to listen empathically, you must be willing to experience something that was overwhelming for her. Just listening can be traumatizing, so you may want to shut down the same way she did. But you must overcome this urge within yourself just as she must try to overcome it within herself. The process of talking about the traumatic emotions is a personal challenge for *both* you and your loved one.

Denial

In your efforts to help your loved one put the trauma behind him, you may unwittingly contribute to his failure to recover—by minimizing the extent of his traumatization. Like Debbie's family, you might focus on his successful survival and pay too little attention to the symptoms he manifests. *Denial* is a psychological mechanism that people sometimes employ in dealing with upsetting situations. Basically, they tell themselves and others that an upsetting situation is simply not that upsetting. Thus, they deny the impact of the situation and, in a sense, try to think of it as a minor thing in order to *make* it a minor thing. We see denial all the time. It's the child who screams, "I'm not angry." It's the depressed adult who claims that the loss of his job doesn't really bother him. It's John Wayne claiming that it's nothing but a minor flesh wound—just before he faints. And it's the rape victim who says she isn't uptight about men, she's just too busy to date anymore.

Denial, in itself, isn't necessarily bad. It's one of the many ways we cope with life's traumas. But denial can become an impediment to your coming to terms with something, such as a loss, that's too big to go away. It's generally no big deal if you deny the impact of the little losses. But the bigger the loss, the more you'll need to acknowledge its impact in order to make adjustments and carry on. If you deny the impact of a major loss, you're unable to recognize your need to either replace what was lost or learn to live without it. Part of coping effectively is being able to *change*. And if you're too immersed in denial, you're blinded to your need to change.

I'm not advocating that you confront any and all of your loved one's denial. It's a normal coping process, and most people who've been traumatized do deny the extent of their traumatization at times. But if it becomes your loved one's sole means of dealing with the trauma, then she's at risk. Moreover, denial has a sort of communicable quality. If your loved one is dealing with her trauma by denying that it had any great impact, there's pressure on you to join in that denial and not disrupt her way of dealing with her trauma. So you don't talk about it, or at least you don't talk about it in any way that will cause her to get upset.

Prospects for recovery are made much worse when the entire family joins with the traumatized member in denying the impact of the trauma. In effect, they perpetuate the idea that the trauma left no lasting psychological scars. Some families don't allow themselves to recognize psychological damage. For them, life is a simple pursuit, and people who have problems are viewed with suspicion, as lazy or weak.

I suspect that most families who live in a permanent world of denial have some kind of unresolved trauma in their past. Frequently, members of such families make comments like, "I saw my father die a violent death when I was a kid, and it didn't 'traumatize' me." Alcoholism is also very common in families that deny the psychological impact of trauma. The alcoholism serves as a form of chemical denial; if they can't talk themselves into *feeling* that the trauma didn't bother them, they can anesthetize the feelings and at least *believe* it didn't bother them.

If the entire family participates in denying the impact of a traumatic event, the trauma survivor is up against much more than his own reluctance to experience the overwhelming feelings. If his symptoms force him to recognize that he's still carrying the effects of traumatization, he'll find it nearly impossible to do much about it as long as his loved ones continue to deny. He may try to argue with them, but he won't win unless other family members support him. He may withdraw from the family and become more symptomatic, or resort to alcohol or drugs. Or he may leave and seek an environment where others will not deny his problems.

The survivor has the best chance for recovery when loved ones don't deny the impact that his traumatization has wrought upon him. One of the most important characteristics of in-patient hospital programs to treat stress disorders is that the staff refuse to join with the patient in denying the seriousness of the traumatization.

Although denial can be used to avoid any emotion or experience, it is most frequently used in regard to *loss*. Traumatization always involves some kind of loss—at the very least, a loss of beliefs (such as an illusion of security), attitudes (such as trust), meaning, and feelings of control. More often, there's a loss of dreams, of innocence, and of the basic sense of self. And sometimes, there are losses of actual people and physical abilities. The main problem with failing to acknowledge loss is that it interferes with the process of adapting, changing, and creating new avenues of fulfillment to replace the ones that are lost.

Wanda, thirty-four, sought therapy because of a lack of fulfillment in her life; she was depressed and had the "blahs." Nothing really excited her, but nothing really got her down either. Wanda's mother had committed suicide when Wanda was seventeen years old. It was a violent suicide, and Wanda had discovered the body. But from all indications, no one in Wanda's family had acknowledged the impact of this terrible event on her. Very little sadness was ever expressed—Wanda herself hadn't cried since the funeral —and the family avoided discussing what had happened. They simply "took it in stride" and continued their lives as they'd been before.

The key point here is that the family members tried to continue their lives as they'd been before. Wanda had been about to get her driver's license and was enrolled to start college. But she never got the license, and she didn't finish the first semester of college. Her brother and sisters also seemed to get stuck at that point in their lives. The family members spent a lot of time together, but they had very little sense of what was going on with one another. At age thirty-four, Wanda began to change this through therapy, making a start by getting her father to give her driving lessons. Then other family members began to liven up a little, and Wanda decided to take more responsibility for bringing the family together, planning some holiday activities that they hadn't pursued since before her mother's death.

One thing Wanda's family hadn't done since the mother's death was to make Christmas cookies, so Wanda announced that she was going to make some. But her attempt turned out to be a disaster—her cookies were nothing like the wonderful ones that her mother used to make. Her mother seemed to be the only person who could bake Christmas cookies, and Wanda cried for the first time since the funeral seventeen years before.

Everyone in Wanda's family had denied the impact of her mother's death and consequently had never really dealt with the loss. Their failure to mourn and share their feelings of loss with one another had caused them to become emo-

tionally numb and distant. And as the episode with the cookies so painfully illustrates, their denial of their loss prevented
them from being able to adapt to it and replace the functions
mother had served for the family. Only when Wanda finally
attempted to replace one of mother's functions did her denial
shatter, and she experienced the tremendous loss. As you can
see, failure to acknowledge loss leads to failure to adapt to it
and replace what was lost.

Protecting the Traumatized Member

You may fail to focus on your loved one's traumatization
because of your own denial and/or because of your reluctance to feel the traumatic emotions, but most likely your
actions are intended to spare your loved one from reliving
his or her intense feelings. You don't want to upset him, and
you may think he'll forget the trauma in time and that it's
best just to leave it be. In some cases, your loved one will
adjust without delving into the trauma. But in most in-
stances, he won't adjust; he'll continue to reexperience the
trauma and will remain emotionally numb and withdrawn.
And as we've seen, many people seem to adjust and have no
symptoms until suddenly, after many years, they appear.

If your family tends to deal with your traumatized loved
one through denial and distancing from the traumatic emotions, your family is likely to be trying to protect the traumatized member. You may form a sort of protective shield
between him and the rest of the world, like an offensive line
surrounding a quarterback. You don't let him encounter
things that are going to be too upsetting, particularly those
that will stir up the traumatic emotions. Jacob Lindy, a psychoanalyst who specializes in the treatment of trauma disorders, refers to this shield as the *trauma membrane*. He says a
traumatized person, in a sense, forms a membrane around
the memories and emotions associated with the trauma. The
family and loved ones become part of that shield.

A trauma membrane is *not* a bad thing—it's a healthy

and caring response to someone who's hurt. When you place a bandage on a wound, you're protecting the hurt from further injury. But there comes a time when it's important to remove the bandage or artificial membrane so that the wound can continue to heal. A cast protects a broken leg to allow it to heal, but if it isn't removed, it interferes with further healing and causes the leg muscles to atrophy and become weaker. If your family relies upon denial and avoids traumatic emotions beyond the time it's healthy, they are likely to maintain the trauma membrane beyond the point where it's helpful.

The trauma membrane is maintained in obvious, visible ways and in subtle, invisible ways. On the obvious level, you may insist that your loved one is "not ready" to do this or that. But you may, in fact, be treating her as if she were a child. This creates resentment in your loved one and can have the same effect as the cast left on the leg too long; her ability to deal with "life"—particularly reminders of the trauma—atrophies, and she comes to doubt herself. On a more subtle level, you avoid certain topics—again, reminders of the trauma—and fail to acknowledge her visible symptoms. In effect, you've altered your expectations of her and, whether in an obvious or a subtle manner, her expectations of herself will begin to change and she'll start to doubt her abilities.

Marsha, Gary, and Suzanne's response to Philip's traumatization is a good example of the creation of a trauma membrane. After their initial, futile efforts to get him to talk about what was bothering him, they learned to back off. The situation reached the point that Philip became noncommunicative and sat in front of the TV for hours, and no one would comment on it or question what was going on. It was as if there were an elephant in the living room, and everyone was acting as if it weren't there at all. Nothing was demanded or expected of Philip—he was free to turn into a hermit in his own house.

This family is an extreme example, but they exemplify processes that occur in many traumatized families. Their reaction to Philip's withdrawn state resembles the fable of the emperor's new clothes. Everyone denies what they're seeing until a small child speaks the truth. This is an excellent story about denial and how it can collapse if people are willing to accept reality. Sometimes we need an innocent child—perhaps that's a service you can perform for your family.

Consider what it would be like to be Gary or Suzanne, living in a situation where there is an elephant in the living room and no one acknowledges that they see it. How does this affect the child, or the adult, who resides in that same living room?

You should now have a solid grasp of what happens when a person is traumatized, both to the individual and to those who are close to him or her. It may have been disturbing to read about all the things that can go wrong. But have hope—the traumatization is only part of the trauma response. There's also a natural process of recovery. Part II will provide you with many specific things you can do to improve and make the most of that healing process.

Part II

HELPING

4

THE RECOVERY PROCESS
An Overview

Part II of this book is about recovery—how it happens and how you can help make it happen. This chapter paints the overall picture of the healing process. I'll address the essentials from the point of view of the different people involved in the ensuing chapters. Chapter 5 is for the actual trauma survivors, and Chapter 6 is for the loved ones, Chapter 7 is for parents of traumatized children. But this chapter provides the overall game plan for recovery. You may want to refer back to this chapter at times in order to understand how the parts fit into the whole.

Aspects of Recovery

William, the survivor who went through the recovery process while living on a commune, did not make his healing journey alone, as we saw in Chapter 1. He had the help of several close friends and a community of caring, understanding people. It's very difficult to make the healing journey without such help from other people. Loved ones provide a sheltered place where the survivor can slowly come to terms with what's happened to her and turn her attention to rebuilding her sense of self. Helpful, understanding people who care are the backbone of the recovery environment.

The Recovery Environment

A trauma response consists of both the damage to the self (the traumatization) and the rebuilding of the self (the recovery). In order to recover, the traumatized person must resolve the primary and the secondary traumas—that is, her unfinished emotional response to the traumatic experience, the deterioration of her relationships with others, and the damage to her sense of self. But recovery from traumatization is a unified experience. It's often arbitrary, even impossible, to separate overcoming the primary trauma from overcoming the secondary trauma.

Although we talk about an individual's recovery as if it took place in isolation, the truth is that the recovering survivor must be seen in the context of his significant relationships, which I lump under the term *family*. Not to do so would be like talking about a fish without acknowledging that it lives in water. So as we look at the recovery process in terms of its individual components, remember that they are all interrelated in a family system.

Overcoming the Primary Trauma

I've emphasized the importance of being able to express a full range of emotions in talking about the buried feelings that are part of the primary trauma. That process is called *catharsis*, and it sometimes brings a release of tensions. But the solution to the primary trauma is *not* simply to express all the feelings associated with it. Although a catharsis of the buried emotions can be a significant part of the solution, it is not the end-all solution to the primary trauma. Resolving the primary trauma is more like a change of attitude than an emotional peak. It means finding a way to think and feel about the trauma that makes it bearable, finding a way to get it into perspective. If you can find a way to make sense of what happened, you'll be able to put the feelings to rest and look ahead at life instead of back at the trauma.

The idea of finding a suitable meaning for one's trauma may seem a little esoteric. What does it mean to find a meaning or create a meaning? This very personal process is unique to every person who undergoes it. A suitable meaning for many people is that "it was God's will." Yet even a common religious explanation can mean something different to different people because no two people have precisely the same worldview. Loved ones and others who wish to help a traumatized person by sharing their personal meanings must do so with an understanding of these differences. Ultimately, the trauma survivor will find his own meaning.

How? Well, he had a meaning for his life before he was traumatized. He had some way of understanding what it's all about, some way of making sense of the whole life experience. Everyone struggles with these questions, and some of us probe more deeply than others. Trauma survivors and their loved ones are forced to probe deeper than most.

Many people who've been traumatized report that the meaning of their entire existence changed as a result of their traumatization. You're probably familiar with stories of combat veterans who return to their homes and become pacifists, ministers, and other sorts of humanitarians. Or the parents of children who've died or suffered—such as those involved in drunk driving, cults, or drugs—who become crusaders against these sources of trauma. Literature is full of inspirational stories about persons who were traumatized, then devoted their lives to something. These persons' traumatization led them to probe more deeply and find new meanings for their lives.

Most trauma survivors, however, don't find new meaning for their entire existence. They simply find a suitable meaning for the traumatization, a view of it that allows them to accept and live with it and what it did to them. They find new ways of viewing themselves and the world they live in; in other words, they change their worldview. But accepting what happened doesn't mean becoming passive—it means letting go, giving up the preoccupation with the past and focusing on the present and the future. An athlete who loses the use of his legs can view himself as a former athlete who can't perform anymore, or he can view himself as a man who doesn't have the use of his legs and therefore must find other avenues of fulfillment in life. The difference is simply one of attitude, but its impact on the quality of life is profound.

A change in attitude is intellectual, but the process that leads to it can be quite emotional. You must accept the emotions that are associated with your trauma, and that means you must overcome your numbing in order to be able to experience those feelings. You must talk about the trauma and its meaning, as well as the feelings. Some people are apparently able to have this talk with themselves, and they manage to change their perspective. But most people can't change their own perspective; they need someone else's perspective to balance their inner dialogue. And you can only let yourself be influenced by someone else's perspective if you trust them. At times the discussion will be very emotional. It will take place more than once, maybe many times. But over time, you can acquire a different perspective on yourself and what you've been through.

Overcoming the Secondary Trauma

Although the secondary trauma is reflected in your relationships, it is, at heart, a damaged sense of self. You feel changed from who and what you were before the trauma. The damage to your sense of self is worsened if you get a poor response from others. The more different you feel—from others and from your former self—the more you'll be likely to withdraw. If others fail to address your trauma, your traumatic thoughts and feelings will become more ensconced behind your trauma membrane. You'll feel even more different and distant from others, and the secondary trauma will take on a life of its own.

You can tell that you are overcoming the secondary trauma when your social sphere starts to expand. That doesn't mean that you become highly social or necessarily have more friends; it means that you begin to experience a greater feeling of belonging. Along with the positive changes in your feelings about others, your feelings about yourself improve. You become more accepting of yourself, and you're calmer and more stable, less easily swayed by emotional tides.

A damaged sense of self is repaired primarily by involvement with people who are accepting, understanding, sympathetic, and willing to deal with your unsavory feelings. In order for a relationship to work, you have to trust the other person. If you trust someone, you let that person matter to you. You care about what she thinks and feels. You give her the power to influence you, to lead you to change at the very core of your personality, to think and feel differently about yourself. When you allow a relationship to become that important, it can help mend your wounded sense of self. But misused, a trust relationship can also cause severe damage.

In the course of repairing your damaged sense of self, you renew your values and restore your faith in yourself and in others. You may redefine your relationship with your social world. Your self-esteem returns, and you can see your basic worth as a human being. Your standards for self-acceptance and acceptance of others usually becomes more flexible and humane. Your sense of having some control over your environment also returns, and your moods stabilize. All these things can happen if you invest yourself in a *healthy* trust relationship.

A healthy trust relationship is one in which difficult feelings are discussed instead of avoided or acted out. This includes your feelings about yourself and about your listener, such as whether you feel you're being understood. You and your listener must be able to tolerate discussing your feelings about each other. Family members often delude themselves into believing that they freely discuss all their feelings about one another, but they often operate according to the unwritten rules discussed in Chapter 3. It's these old, restrictive rules that have to give way, since it's hard to reveal one's true feelings in a judgmental atmosphere.

Grieving the Losses

A significant part of the recovery process is grieving for the many losses associated with the traumatization. These include physical losses, a lost sense of security, lost dreams and innocence, lost relationships, lost years, and the loss of whoever you were before and whoever you hoped to be. For each trauma survivor, there are surely more losses as well. Grieving these many losses is an important part of letting go of the past and turning to the future because once the past is grieved, it can be relinquished.

Different people grieve differently. Some people grieve very visibly, others quietly. Some people put considerable time into it; others think about the loss only occasionally. One way or another, you must allow yourself to experience the emotions and think deeply about your loss and what it means to you. This generally means *talking* about what you've lost. Although some people seem to be able to have that conversation with themselves, most of us need another human ear.

Creating a New Niche

A niche is a situation or activity that's especially suited to your abilities or character. The longer you are affected by a trauma before resolving it, the more you'll gravitate toward a niche that fits your traumatization. You'll be caught up in a life-style that serves to help you deal with your symptoms and avoid your painful feelings. Some of these life-styles are more destructive than others. You've lost your old niche, and even if you have created another new one, it's likely to have elements that support your avoidance of your trauma. Recovering requires you to build yet another new niche. This can mean anything from changing your habits to changing your job to changing your friends.

The most important part of your niche is the group of people with whom you're intimate—your family, lovers, and close friends. These are the people who must provide the support; their opinions and tolerance affect your secondary trauma and its resolution. If they care about you and have healthy trust relationships with you, the necessary conditions for your recovery environment are there. But you must make efforts to actively change your life-style and to carve out a new, healthier niche. The interpersonal changes—whether finding new friends or new ways of relating to old friends and loved ones—are usually the most difficult changes involved in creating a new niche.

Dealing with the Rage

One aspect of traumatization that many people try to avoid is rage. Rage is an emotion that other people sense and avoid; you're generally at a loss as how to handle it. You may even hide your rage from yourself as well as others so that you may see it only indirectly, through your attitudes or the way you drive. Or it may be easier to hold the distorted view that *others* are the enraged ones and you're only a victim. But at some level, most victims are enraged at what has happened to them.

Learning to deal with your rage means learning to express it, examine it, and experience it without acting it out. The goal is not to simply "get the rage out"—that only tends to lead to more rage. Rather, the goal is to understand it, to accept the rage and see if anything can be done about the circumstances that provoked it. This is not easy to do—our society always has difficulty dealing with anger.

Your rage about your traumatization is primarily a reaction to your feelings of helplessness. A combination of intense anger and frustration may produce a fleeting feeling of power that combats the feeling of helplessness. Yet the rage frightens everyone, including you (though you might deny it because you're emotionally numb). Some people are so frightened of their own rage that they can allow themselves to experience it only when they're intoxicated and therefore unable to control it. In Chapter 9, we'll talk more about overcoming rage.

Dealing with Earlier Traumas

Unfortunately, traumatization often uncovers earlier problems that have to be dealt with before recovery is complete. An earlier trauma is often brought back to life by a second traumatization, especially if there are common elements. This means the earlier trauma must also be resolved in the course of recovery. Commonly, the kinds of childhood issues that people generally work on in psychotherapy are apt to be a part of the recovery process.

Dealing with Moods and Physical Symptoms

Recovery is difficult, even if you have energy and can apply yourself diligently to the work of recovering. But it's much harder if you're depressed, are not getting adequate sleep, or are preoccupied with other physical symptoms and anxieties. Emotional improvement generally leads to physical improvements, but physical factors—such as depression and physical aches and pains—can prevent emotional work from moving forward. So the emotional work of recovery—which largely occurs in relationships—should be accompanied by work on the physical symptoms associated with depression, anxiety, and hyperarousal. This second kind of work, which we will focus on in Chapter 8, can include diet and exercise, changes in sleeping patterns, and other efforts to get control of one's physical existence.

Tasks and Rituals

There are a number of things that trauma survivors and their loved ones can do to facilitate the recovery process. I've emphasized talking openly and honestly about painful issues, the meaning of the trauma, and the feelings that exist between the survivor and the listener. This should become a regular habit, not just a scheduled event. If you discuss your feelings openly, you'll learn to process your life as you experience it. This allows you to deal with upsetting details as they emerge rather than storing the reactions until they build into more powerful fears.

With tasks and rituals (which I'll describe in detail in Chapter 10) this experiencing process can occur in a manner that is directly related to your traumatization. It's hard to feel completely alone with a loss if you go through a ritual—such as a funeral—with a large group of people who share the feeling and process it together in some kind of ritualized form.

Stages of Recovery

It's popular to discuss recovery in terms of stages, whether it's recovery from trauma, illness, or any other setback. For years, theories about loss—marked by stages like denial, anger, and bargaining—dominated our way of looking at the grieving process. But stage theories of recovery can be misleading. People read that they're supposed to go through such and such stages in such and such an order, and they can come to feel that something's wrong with them if that's not the way it happens for them. There was always a group of people who didn't fit the stages, and this can contribute to a point of view that regards these people as not grieving. Instead, it appears that they are grieving in different ways. At best, stages describe the more common experiences. Like statistics, they're useful for describing large groups, but they're limited when applied to an individual.

So as I describe the natural order of the recovery events I've discussed in this chapter, bear in mind that some of you will not follow the order I suggest, and others won't experience *all* the events. More often than not, you'll be dealing with several of these "stages" at once.

The Primary Trauma Stage

The two primary trauma symptoms, reexperiencing and emotional numbing, are usually cyclic in nature. Their cycle can be interrupted if you stop the emotional numbing and stay with the feelings more. This doesn't mean the numbing suddenly stops—at times of stress, you may resort to it again. But numbing can become less pervasive, and as it diminishes, the reexperiencing symptom takes on a different form. You choose to examine and thus reexperience; as a choice, it feels more under control. Your examination of your suppressed thoughts and feelings becomes more intense, and you avoid your intrusive memories less—they're expressed, examined, and accepted. This examination process leads to changes in your attitude and your feelings about the primary trauma.

The Secondary Trauma Stage

The secondary trauma usually takes the form of a steady withdrawal from wider circles of social belonging. You bury yourself in the innermost concentric rings of your social sphere. Recovery reverses this and generally proceeds from your inner, most intimate groups to your outer, more distant ones. The most important step tends to be the first one— allowing some individual or group to become important to you once again. When you find an intimate and highly supportive situation where you can be honest and vulnerable, you can express and examine the thoughts and feelings related to your primary trauma. The secondary trauma "stage" can't be entirely separated from the primary trauma stage. These close encounters with others eventually lead to changes in the way you think and feel about yourself and your world.

Initial Blocks

Often, you cannot really start your recovery until you overcome your inability to express your grief. Some trauma survivors won't be able to form a significant trust relationship until they have developed some control over their rage. Debilitating moods and physical symptoms must be improved before many survivors can devote energy to the other work of recovery. You'll continue working on grief, rage, moods, and physical symptoms throughout the recovery process, but initially they can form a block that must be acknowledged and addressed before other issues can receive attention.

Changing Niches

For most trauma survivors, the changing of the niche occurs during the middle and later phases of recovery. The old niche tends to be one where you no longer feel safe enough to reveal your more tender feelings; the new niche is one where hopefully you do.

Pursuing Tasks and Rituals

Just to be clear, tasks and rituals don't constitute a recovery stage per se. Rather, they accompany the other aspects of recovery, and you can use them to try to bring certain elements of recovery to a head. Rituals often mark transition points, so they may be particularly visible at certain points in the recovery process. Tasks and rituals occur all the way through the recovery process, though their nature may change as recovering proceeds.

Resolving Earlier Traumas

Earlier traumas tend to be uncovered during the middle and later phases of recovery. The resolution of earlier trauma can be one of the last things that occurs in the recovery process. If you're in psychotherapy, you may be interested in continuing in therapy beyond the resolution of the current trauma so that you can work further on these issues.

Recovery begins with reexperiencing and reexamining the primary trauma. It's completed when you've recovered your sense of self and feel a sense of belonging to the wider segments of society. The journey between these two points can be a lengthy one; I hope you can start feeling better as soon as you recognize that your journey toward recovery has actually begun.

5

GUIDELINES FOR THE
TRAUMA SURVIVOR
Reaching Out/Delving Within

This chapter is for those who are actually trauma survivors. Whether you know it or not, you're already doing things to cope with your suffering. You're coping with daily stress, and with the symptoms and problems that your traumatization has produced. The things you're doing may be helping but not enough; worse yet, some of the ways you're coping may be producing additional problems.

Coping with Daily Stress

A stressor is something that produces stress. It may be the traffic on the freeway, friction with your boss, or the intrusive memory of a trauma. All of these produce stress, some more than others. When you encounter a minor or major stressor, you put your coping mechanisms to work. If it's a major stressor, you likely put more of them to work, including those you don't often use in dealing with the minor stressors. We all have those coping mechanisms that we rely upon regularly, and we have others that we maintain in reserve for major stressful events, such as the loss of a loved one.

Many of the coping mechanisms you use for minor stressors in your daily life are limited in their power. They are not adequate for major stressors, providing short-term help at best. You get into trouble if you try to stretch some of these minor strategies to fit situations that are too much for them. These daily mechanisms are very important, to be sure —they're the foundation of your coping style, and they reflect your basic attitude about how you view and deal with stressful events. Some people confront stressors, while others avoid them. You probably do some of both, but if you always avoid daily stressors, you'll be at a disadvantage in dealing with major stressors.

Your Coping Style

At this point, stop and take the time to assess your own coping style. Write down a few sentences that describe your approach to dealing with stressors, both major and minor. Here are some questions to consider:

- What are your predominant attitudes about daily stress? Is it best to confront it or avoid it?

- What kinds of things have you done in the past to deal with major stressors? Have you ever numbed out? If so, how much? Have you ever been a sensation or arousal seeker, or put yourself in situations that recreate your trauma? Again, how often? Have you ever pursued a program of self-discipline? If so, how far did it go? Was it useful?

- How much have you effectively used recreation, relaxation, or exercise to deal with stress?

Your coping style is strongly influenced by your family background. Stop and think about it—What's your family's coping style? Here are some more questions to consider:

- Do you come from a family that encourages ignoring daily stresses? Or does your family help you recognize and anticipate life's problems? Do they accept problems as challenges?

- Is it acceptable to talk about problems in your family, even little ones? Or is it frowned upon and viewed as whining or feeling sorry for yourself?

- Think back to your family's unwritten rules about expressing emotion. Is it *really* permitted to get upset about something that happens to you?

- How does your personal coping style mesh with your family's unwritten rules?

- Are you still following the same rules you grew up with, or have you reacted against some rules by trying to live very differently?

There are as many ways of coping with daily-life stress as there are kinds of people. But there are some common patterns, and you're likely to approach traumatic stress in one of these ways. Here are some of the common attitudes people adopt toward daily stress.

Ignore It

One of the most common ways of dealing with stress is to do nothing whatsoever. Act as if it doesn't bother you, and the theory is that it won't. This is the John Wayne approach, strong and silent. You probably use this coping mechanism sometimes since the best way to deal with many of life's minor stressors is, in fact, to ignore them. But pretending that a major stressor doesn't bother you generally doesn't work— major stressors are hard to ignore. Ignoring them (stoicism) can block the all-important processing that is needed in the case of trauma.

Forget It

Another coping mechanism that you probably use is to try to forget what happened. Sometimes people are able to leave traumas behind them. Even in major traumas, most people have a healthy tendency to forget things that are too disturbing, such as the grisly details. Over time, you're able to forget many aspects of a major trauma. You generally don't forget that it happened, but you're often able to forget many of the little memory cues that bring back the worst of it.

Sneer at It

Some people regard life's stresses as a challenge and respond to them by becoming aggressive and competitive. This is a way of dealing with the trauma *directly*, rather than avoiding it by ignoring or forgetting it. Football players sneer at and ignore stressors when they overcome minor injuries and go back on the field to win. The spirit behind this attitude can get you through many a jam, but you need more than this to deal with a serious trauma.

Laugh It Off

A sense of humor is one of the blessings we've been given to deal with the frustrations and disappointments of life. It plays a part in helping us change our perspective and reduce the sting of events. It's one of the very best coping mechanisms you can have, but it's still only one of a number of mechanisms that you need in order to deal with a major trauma.

Talk About It

Many people cope with daily stress by talking about it and sharing their feelings about it with others. This serves to decrease the pressure they're under and provides the opportunity for a change of perspective. Talking about stress is a mainstay coping strategy; you can use it with the smallest stressors and the major ones. It's primarily through talking that you examine and change your perspective. It's also through talking that you express your feelings and, in the process, come to understand them more clearly yourself. Through talking with someone you trust and care about, you can process and ultimately come to terms with traumatization.

Coping with Traumatic Stress

These basic attitudes about daily stress influence how a person will approach major forms of stress. In general, people need more powerful, long-term coping mechanisms when they are dealing with major stressors, particularly when they've been traumatized. The following are some mechanisms that people commonly use to deal with a trauma.

Numbing Out

Most people numb out their emotions and stop feeling them at some point in dealing with traumatic stress. But doing this creates a host of other problems. Since numbing out is difficult for some people, they may resort to drugs and alcohol to help them numb out. Once you've numbed out sufficiently, you carry an emotional deadness inside; then you resort to further problematic mechanisms to overcome the deadness.

It is sometimes adaptive to be able to numb out, and people who function at a high level in crisis situations are usually good at numbing. But it becomes a major symptom of PTSD if it goes too far.

Sharon was an emergency-room nurse who overdid her emotional numbing. When she started ER work, she learned to maintain emotional distance in dealing with trauma victims. Sometimes she and the other ER staff would even gather in the staff lounge and make fun of the misery of the traumatized patients. Sharon initially found this to be cruel, and she held back during the joking. But after a while, it didn't seem so bad to her, and she found she was comfortable with it even though she still cared deeply about the people she treated.

Then Sharon's hospital was elevated in the trauma network of major hospitals in her city. The hospital nearest hers closed down its trauma services, and suddenly Sharon's ER was barraged with additional patients, including many victims of violent crime from a part of town that the other hospital had previously served. Her job changed its character. Every shift was enormously draining; everyone felt overworked. For Sharon, it meant exposure to many more, very severe injuries.

Sharon found that the depth of her feeling for the patients became shallower. She became hardened, and the humor in the lounge was no longer funny—there was a bite to it that hadn't been there before. Sharon and many of her colleagues had become emotionally numb, and she even developed a drinking problem. A therapist recognized that she'd been traumatized and helped her stop drinking. Sharon then transferred to a different section of the hospital and recovered her emotional spontaneity.

Sensation-Seeking

Sensation-seeking is a means of coping with the deadness that comes from excessive numbing out. Sensation-seekers and "adrenaline junkies" pursue high-risk activities to give themselves a jolt to overcome their lack of feeling. They may work in high-risk professions, have high-risk hobbies, or lead dangerous lives. We all enjoy some occasional excitement in our lives, but sensation-seekers' lives center on getting that excitement. Without it, they feel empty and depressed. The following example of a sensation-seeker may seem exaggerated, but there are a surprising number of trauma survivors who live just like this man.

Sam was traumatized in Vietnam. He was in bitter fighting and faced death a number of times. Back in the States, he became a policeman. He always managed to be involved in the more severe incidents, and he fought with several desperate criminals. In his off-duty hours, he rode a motorcycle, drank heavily, and often got into fights at bars, usually with much bigger opponents. His hobbies were whitewater kayaking, rock climbing, and sky-diving. Seldom did a week go by when Sam didn't have a major adrenaline rush over something, much as he had during his perilous tour of combat duty. The risk-taking nature of Sam's sensation-seeking may represent more than just an effort to overcome inner deadness. Many sensation-seekers also have survivor guilt (see page 55) and are testing their fate and punishing themselves.

Arousal-Seeking

Arousal-seeking includes not only sensation-seeking but less risky activities as well. Arousal-seekers work to keep themselves on an adrenaline high. Some work at an intense job, while others resort to drug use, sexual addiction, and fighting. They use the arousing quality of these experiences either to keep themselves from feeling deadness inside or to find outlets for the state of hyperarousal that their traumatization has produced.

Marian, who was physically and sexually abused by her mother's boyfriends and a stepfather, grew up feeling deadened inside. As an adolescent, she used every drug that came along and became particularly fond of amphetamines, which gave her a feeling of being very up and intense. As an adult, she relinquished most of her drug use, but became obsessed with sex and slept with several men each week. She couldn't tolerate sitting around her home and went out virtually every night. She eventually got control of her sexual behavior but became deeply involved with her career, working long days and taking little time to herself. One way or another, this arousal-seeker always kept herself going at a high pitch.

Pursue a Program of Self-Discipline

Many people stave off the effects of traumatization by undergoing a self-imposed program that requires high levels of self-discipline. It may be an exercise program, a work project, or an intensely preoccupying hobby. When Marian went from purely arousing activities to an intense investment in her work, it allowed her to focus her high level of energy, but she was still burning herself up. There's a fine line between a healthy program of self-discipline and an obsession that runs your life.

Chris grew up in a violent, alcoholic family. Her father beat her when she disobeyed or challenged him about his drinking. She also saw him beat her mother several times. She never felt protected in her family. Chris coped by becoming highly involved in athletics at school. She was quite driven in her devotion to practice and became an accomplished gymnast, which eventually earned her a scholarship. After college she moved away from her family. But she continued to pursue athletic activities to such a degree that it created new problems. When she damaged her knees by running enormous distances each week, she switched to swimming and tennis. When she gained weight in her late twenties, she became obsessed with her diet and nearly starved herself. She eventually went to a program for eating disorders and learned to be less rigid in her pursuit of programs that were supposed to make her feel better.

Relive the Trauma

Some people work to overcome the effects of traumatization by exposing themselves to the trauma repeatedly until it loses its power over them. They may be so intent on doing this that they go out of their way to recreate and relive the trauma. Whenever they encounter a situation that reminds them of the trauma, they feel compelled to enter the situation and master the feelings it evokes.

Emma's father drank and beat his wife and children. She left home when she was eighteen years old by running away with a boy and getting married. The marriage lasted less than two years; after that, Emma became involved in two different relationships with men who battered her. She left each of the men and went to live elsewhere several times, but she invariably returned to the men who mistreated her. She felt she could help these men overcome their tendency to beat her by becoming more accepting and understanding of them. Only after she realized she was still trying to change her abusive father was she able to feel appropriately frightened, leave these abusive men, and get involved with a nonabusive man.

Dealing with the Meaning of Your Trauma

These mechanisms are some common ways people deal with the disturbing emotions stirred up by their traumatization. You probably recognize some of them yourself. But ultimately, you must deal with the *meaning* of your traumatization. Only then will you come to terms with it and be able to live with it. Here are some of the ways you can make sense of what's happened to you.

Change Your Perspective

We often overcome our upset at one of life's obstacles by telling ourselves that it's not such a big thing. This coping mechanism is reflected in the aphorism, "I cried because I had no shoes, until I saw a man who had no feet." By changing your perspective on the severity of the trauma, you change its meaning and therefore diminish its power over you.

While Judy was looking for work in the field of modeling, she was involved in an automobile accident that resulted in a nasty scar on her face. Naturally, she felt her life was ruined. She became depressed and bitter and lost her motivation, saying that this was God's way of telling her that she was too vain and that now she would be forced to know what it felt like to be ugly and to envy the beautiful people. Judy's family talked her into getting plastic surgery. She had two operations, and both times she criticized the results. Although the surgeries brought some improvement, they didn't make the scar invisible.

One day, one of Judy's old high school girlfriends talked her into helping out at the day-care center where she worked. Judy discovered she enjoyed working with children, perhaps in part because some of them openly asked about her scar but didn't seem to be put off by it. Her interest grew, and she eventually sought a degree in early childhood education. She had found a goal that gave her life meaning once more.

Today, Judy is happy; she isn't obsessed with her scar or what happened to her. She no longer feels that the accident was meant to teach her anything. She still wishes that it had never happened but adds that it may have been a blessing in disguise. Although when it first happened, she felt she was ugly, now she doesn't think so. She looks in the mirror and sees herself, not her scar. And the blessing is that now this is how she looks at other people too. In coming to terms with her traumatization, Judy's perspective has changed, and she has grown.

You can work on changing your perspective by doing the following:

- Talk to someone you trust. Is there anyone you can talk to who has been through a similar experience? Whoever you talk to, let them know how you feel, how you view what's happened to you.

- If there's no one with whom you can talk about these things, find a good therapist. (See Chapter 12 for guidelines).

- Verbalize the questions that are plaguing you. See what answers others might have for those questions. Their answers don't have to be your answers, but they may bring you a new perspective.

- Tell the people you trust about your losses. Accept their support. Don't pretend that it doesn't matter.

- Explore the ways you've changed. Who were you before? Who are you now? What are the things that make you feel good about yourself? What makes you feel bad about yourself?

- See if you can describe your worldview. Take some time and spell it out in detail. How has it changed from what it was before?

- What have you learned from your traumatization? What would you now want to teach your children of your experience?

- What benefits? What do you have now that you didn't have before?

Strengthen Your Belief System

One common result of traumatization is that people's belief systems change. Existing beliefs become stronger, or new beliefs may replace old ones. This can give you greater strength to cope with both the primary and secondary traumas.

Many people find religion as a result of being traumatized; of course this is not the only way a person might change his beliefs. Traumatization causes you to ask questions—about yourself, your life, even the meaning of existence. You need solid answers when you've been traumatized, not superficial ones. You may come up with the same answers you had before, but they're probably more deeply thought out. Or you may have to find answers to questions you really hadn't considered before.

Beliefs are often strengthened when a person is recovering from shattered illusions and is consciously reexamining his or her most basic beliefs. It's not so much a coping strategy as a by-product of the process of examination. But as beliefs strengthen, they contribute to a person's emotional equilibrium as well as his intellectual stability.

Harriet was eighteen years old when her father lost his temper and became violent in an argument with her mother. He struck her mother with a heavy object and killed her. Harriet hadn't known him to be a particularly violent man, though his temper had always been very hot. When it happened, she was away at her first semester of college, so she didn't directly witness the violence. But the trauma for Harriet was the sudden loss of her mother and the knowledge that her father had done this horrible thing. Her life was turned upside down. She dropped out of school and went to live with some of her mother's close relatives. Just about everyone she encountered viewed her father as evil and discouraged her from seeing him at all. But it was not so simple for Harriet. He was still her father, and now he was the only parent she had.

After eight months, she decided that she needed to visit her father. Several years later, she continues to visit him in prison. Her feelings about him have been all over the map, but she refuses to write him out of her life entirely. She was uncertain about this for some time, but finally she came to believe there was something worthwhile and redeemable about him. She seems to have found some answers to her question about how he could have done what he did to her mother. She realized that he'd always had the potential to do such a thing but that she'd simply made herself believe that it wasn't so. Now her naïveté is gone, but her belief about her father's underlying worth survives. Harriet's beliefs about people in general will never be the same, but she feels she has a grasp of human nature that better prepares her for the worst, yet still lets her enjoy the good in others.

Devote Your Life to a Cause

Many people handle a major traumatization by devoting their lives to a cause, usually one related to the trauma. Organizations such as Mothers Against Drunk Driving are formed by trauma survivors or their loved ones (who are also trauma survivors). Many former addicts devote their lives to helping other addicts kick their habit. And survivors build memorials, such as the Vietnam Veterans Memorial in Washington, in hope of helping other survivors. All these groups give meaning to their lives by helping others. Many traumatized people become crusaders in order to bring meaning into a life that might otherwise feel meaningless. But organized causes are only the more obvious examples—there are also causes that aren't as obvious. Here's an example of someone finding a cause as a way of bringing meaning to her traumatization.

Angela, a clinical psychologist who specializes in "women's issues," is very concerned with "giving women their power," helping those women who've been abused—physically or emotionally—by others, particularly men. She knows that her desire to help the underpowered women in the world stems in large part from her own abuse as a child. She doesn't want anyone else to have to live through what she's experienced. She's given her life meaning by helping others avoid the trauma she endured. In a sense, this allows her to attribute a positive meaning to her own abuse because of the good it's enabled her to do for others.

No one coping style works for everyone. You must start from the kind of coping style you already have and think about ways to improve upon it. Finding causes and deep beliefs is not for everyone, but everyone *does* need to change their perspective. You must take the time to think about what you believe in and what gives your life meaning. You'll probably find that it helps to have someone with whom you can talk about these things—just thinking about them isn't so easy. When I was a freshman at Texas A&M, we weren't permitted to "think" about things; we were told we could only "cogitate." Cogitating means to take careful and leisurely thought, to meditate or ponder, to consider intently. I suggest you "cogitate" about the meaning of your life. Here are some tough questions for you to ponder:

- What are the most important things in your life? Are they things that you already have or do, or are they things that you're striving to attain? If you're not striving for them, why not?
- What are your priorities?
- Do you feel there is a spiritual dimension to life? Are your spiritual needs being met?
- Who are the most important people in your life? Have they always been, or have the important people changed over time?
- What are your personal strengths? What about your weaknesses? Have these changed? If so, what strengths have you lost? Are there things you can do to get them back?
- How do you think you're seen by others? What do they admire about you? What do they see as your weaknesses? How would you like to be viewed by others?
- Who do you consider to be people who are living their lives meaningfully? What prevents you from living your life more like them?
- Is there a purpose to life, to suffering, to loss? How do you account for the existence of terrible things, such as the trauma that you've suffered?
- How do you feel about yourself? Are you the kind of person you want to be?
- Where do you fit in your view of the world? Are you making a contribution?

It can be helpful to project yourself into the future in order to obtain a better perspective on the present. Here are some questions that you can consider:

- When you think about the latter stages of your life, what do you hope to be doing, to have done? What kind of person do you hope to be?

- Imagine yourself at the end of your life. Now look back and think about your trauma response. How did it change your life? What more positive place could that change have led to? How might your trauma response have evolved, both in a more positive direction and a more negative direction?

Processing Your Trauma

As you evaluate yourself and your use of coping mechanisms, you will develop a picture of how you're dealing with your traumatization. You may feel that you're dealing with the symptoms part of the trauma response, but not moving forward with the healing because your perspective has not changed and life feels meaningless. If so, you must closely examine your coping mechanisms. These are what you have the greatest control over! Ask yourself whether you're coping in a manner that allows you to *process* the trauma—or only contain it.

What exactly is processing the trauma? *Processing* is an internal experience in which you examine and reflect upon your feelings, attitudes, and beliefs. It's the process of change. It's usually accompanied by conversation, but the processing shouldn't be confused with the conversation.

It's in your feelings that processing takes place. You continually process feeling states. When your interests or tastes change, you've processed some feelings. Some feelings are much stronger than others, loaded with emotion and hard to change. Feelings related to your traumatization are very strong. But even strong feelings change. The strength of the emotion underlying most feelings fades over time—and facing fears can help diminish their strength.

So look at your coping style and decide whether it's allowing you to process your traumatization. If not, what needs to change?

Reaching Out/Delving Within

As you alter your patterns of coping in order to facilitate your processing, two things need to happen. First, you must find the time and opportunity to delve within and find answers for the questions your traumatization has created. Second, you must reach out and make better contact with your world and the people who populate it. These two events weave around and through one another—often you delve within by reaching out and talking to someone about your inner feelings, beliefs, and attitudes. It's hard to simply talk about feelings, beliefs, and attitudes; you discover those parts of yourself through talking and thinking about *events* in your life.

It's important that you and your loved ones have similar attitudes about the necessity of talking. If you don't, then trying to talk will create new tensions. Don't be too quick to assume that you know what your loved ones' attitudes are, much less your own. Just because no one has been talking doesn't mean that no one wants to. Many families remain silent because each member thinks that this is what everyone else wants. Your first step may be to ask your loved ones how they feel about the whole idea of talking.

The events you need to talk about may be the primary trauma or other aspects of your life that provoke strong feelings. Some people will need to talk explicitly about the trauma. Others will find that they and their loved ones communicate in other ways and don't feel it's necessary to talk about the trauma per se. You may or may not feel it's necessary to talk about the frightening details of your trauma, but even if you do, not everyone has to know them. What is more important is that they understand *what* you're upset about. As long as you feel understood, you've made the connection you need to process your trauma. If you don't feel understood, speak up. That's where the work begins.

6

GUIDELINES FOR LOVED ONES
Talking/Listening/Relating to the Trauma Survivor

At this point, those of you who are involved with a loved one who is a trauma survivor may be feeling pretty helpless yourselves. You may be feeling pulled between joining your loved one in his isolation or abandoning him and going on with your life. You may be resentful and have lost patience with him. You may even have disengaged and broken the connection between you because it's just too difficult to stay tuned in. If you've broken the connection with someone you love, this chapter will provide you with guidelines for reconnecting. And if you've hung in there with a frustrating connection, this chapter will help you deal with many of the obstacles that you're facing. The central issue in improving your connection is communication.

117

Talking to the Trauma Survivor

It should be clear by now that I consider it important for trauma survivors to talk. I don't know what your traumatized loved one needs to talk about; each survivor is different. Most survivors need to talk about their traumatic experiences, but not all. So your first goal may be to convince her that you want to hear what she has to say, and that you want to understand what it's like to be in her shoes.

Your Decision to Talk

If she perceives that you're less than sincere about wanting to talk, she may not talk in a way that will be truly helpful to her. Thus, the first obstacle for you, the listener, to contend with is whether you really *do* want to know what your loved one's traumatic experience was like. Before you go any further, you need to examine whether you are indeed prepared to experience vicariously the awful emotions and details of your loved one's traumatization. If you're uncertain but think you want to try, go ahead—but proceed cautiously. Trauma survivors are extremely sensitive to how much others actually want to *relate* to their feelings and put themselves in their place.

If your self-exploration reveals that you aren't prepared to relate to your loved one's feelings, you must make some decisions. You might want to enter psychotherapy yourself in order to get some support for this task. Or you may be able to find a support group in your community, composed of other people who are dealing with similar issues. Family members can help enormously. But whatever route you choose, don't expect perfection, and don't expect to feel totally able to deal with your loved one's traumatization—that's unrealistic. You are not going to be able to come along and magically cure your loved one. What's more likely to happen is that you and your traumatized loved one are going to explore her feelings together. The decision I'm asking you to make is not whether you think you can handle it all, but whether you're willing to hang in there and try to understand and relate to some very disturbing thoughts and feelings.

But what if you are too depressed yourself? What if you're so angry at your loved one that you can hardly talk openly with him? What if you've had too much emotional turmoil in your own life, and you just don't have any more tolerance? What can you do? To begin with, this is not an all-or-nothing decision. If you can't do it yourself, you can work at making it happen with someone else. But don't be too quick to decide that you're not up to this task. You may not feel ready to leap into the deep end of the pool, but with some guidance you may be ready to inch into the shallow end. It's been my experience that you and your loved one will be able to deal with things better than either of you ever imagined.

His Decision to Talk

If you've come to terms with your reluctance to delve, you must prepare for your talk. Your decision to enter your loved one's world of traumatized emotions will not be a one-time event. It's a decision that you must reexamine and re-make repeatedly as you actually encounter those feelings. It may seem easy to sit here and read about those emotions and believe that you can tolerate them with minimal effort, but it's a different affair to actually experience them directly. It's no accident that so many traumatized people devote their energies to staying away from the emotions associated with the event. It's one thing to talk about the enormous anxiety associated with a near-death experience—it's another to live it.

Now that you've decided to talk about it and know that you'll have to continue to monitor your own reactions, you must open communication with your loved one. He needs to be aware that you want to talk with him about his experience, and he needs to have the opportunity to make a decision to do so himself. If he decides that he doesn't want to discuss it, your goal will change. You must convince him of the benefit of opening up and sharing what he's experienced and is continuing to experience. You must explore his fears about talking. Perhaps he's already tried and found it to be unproductive or even destructive. He may have already experienced the pain of trying to talk and feeling the other person distance from him whenever he approached the traumatic emotions.

More likely than not, however, he'll agree to talk. This doesn't mean he's decided to let you in—only that he's agreed to talk to you about his traumatic experience. Remember that most trauma survivors are adept at talking about their traumatic experience *without* feeling any of the emotions. They can employ their emotional numbing and even discuss the event rather easily without actually feeling anything. So if your loved one is like this, agreeing to talk only means that you're going to have some access to his experience; the real work is still ahead. Other trauma survivors cannot numb out their emotions so easily. For these people, agreeing to talk can actually constitute a decision to let you in. If you've been let in, tread carefully. Bear in mind that your loved one is struggling to control overwhelming emotions.

The Discussion

Once it's accepted that you and your loved one are going to talk about his trauma and what it's done to him, you can do some things to facilitate the discussion. Here are some guidelines to help you establish the right kind of atmosphere so that your loved one feels safe and so that the two (or more) of you are as comfortable as possible.

1. Establish the Setting

It's important to set the scene. Make sure you have sufficient time and a place that is free of distractions and interruptions. You've made it clear to your loved one that you're serious about wanting to talk, so don't contradict that message by choosing a setting that doesn't easily permit serious discussion. We're often tempted to bring up difficult topics at casual moments, when the other person is engaged in an activity such as washing the dishes or driving the car. This can be a way of trying to lighten the atmosphere and avoid the anxiety of facing a difficult topic head-on. But I recommend that you find a time and place that has no distractions and allows face-to-face conversation, to support your contention that you really want to talk.

2. *Ask Questions*

A primary goal of your discussions is for you, the listener, to learn what it was like for your loved one to experience her trauma, and what it's been like for her to live with it since. You want to find out what it feels like to be her and to have lived through what she's lived through. That means you're not there to tell her what it's been like; you're there for her to tell you. She's not there to get advice, and it's probably better not to offer it unless she asks for it. Be careful not to lecture, and don't reassure her that the worst is over with (maybe it's not) or tell her that she shouldn't focus on the past. Your comments should be directed toward *clarifying your understanding* of what she's telling you. Beyond that, you should probably only say enough to keep her talking and to demonstrate that you're following her words carefully.

3. *"I Know Just How You Feel."*

No, you don't. If you try to say that you do, you'll only discredit your assertion that you want to find out how she feels. Instead, don't be afraid to acknowledge your ignorance! She knows that you don't know, and the most important thing to her is your sincere desire to understand what it has felt like for her to go through her trauma. If she doesn't pick up a feeling of sincere desire, she won't be able to open up with you. If you don't understand something, let her know. Make it your *mutual* goal to develop understanding. Your lack of common experience may lead you to push her to provide you with new examples, new metaphors, for what she's experiencing. This can result in her developing a stronger grasp of her own experience, as well as greater understanding in you.

For example, you might say something like: "Look, I know that I haven't been through anything that compares with what you went through. But I really want to know what it was like. I want to know what it's like for you to live with it now. Teach me. Help me understand. I'll listen to anything you have to say about it. I'm interested in anything that you think is relevant. Bear with me—I can learn. And I will, with your help!"

On the other hand, don't be afraid to offer her a comparable experience of your own as part of your effort to understand. The boyfriend of a woman who's been raped, for example, might recall being burglarized and his feeling of discomfort at someone having access to his most private possessions. He could describe this experience as a means of seeking common ground for understanding what her experience was like for her. You may fear that you will minimize her experience by comparing it with something more trivial, but I believe you shouldn't hold back. Sharing an even partly comparable experience is a step in the direction of understanding. The danger is that she might misinterpret your telling the story as an assumption on your part that you already understand, rather than an attempt to move toward better understanding.

To prevent that, the boyfriend might say something like: "I know this must sound trivial in comparison to what you went through, but my house was burglarized once. I felt this sickening feeling, not over what was taken as much as just the thought of some stranger going through my stuff. I'm sure what I felt doesn't begin to come close to what it was like to be raped. But I'm trying to understand what it must have been like for you, and I thought it might be a similar kind of thing. Am I even in the ballpark?"

It's imperative that you make clear that you know you do *not* understand, but that you're searching for a common experience to give yourself a sense of what she's feeling. Most traumatized people are actually not put off when others try to relate to their trauma by comparing it with more trivial experiences—as long as those others are not simply making a token effort at understanding or assuming they understand when they don't. There's an initial disappointment when a survivor discovers that even loved ones don't understand, but I believe that it can be overcome if you persevere and don't let the survivor fall back into her old pattern of not talking.

4. Come to Grips with the Emotions

The primary reason your loved one hasn't already talked through the trauma is that the emotions associated with it are overwhelming. Even approaching them fills him with anxiety and dread. In order to make any headway in examining them, he needs to feel not only that you are with him but that you yourself can tolerate and handle the emotions he's stirring up. Remember, he's used to having people steer him *away* from those feelings and distance themselves from him when he begins to experience them. If you continue to stay linked by concentrating on what he's communicating, then he's likely to go more deeply into his unexplored feelings.

The primary obstacle to maintaining your link with him is your own natural reluctance to experience overwhelming emotions. None of us is immune to this, and at times we're more than reluctant. Some of us just can't do it at all until we overcome emotional blocks within ourselves. Since part of what you're trying to do is to help your loved one overcome an emotional block, you must stay tuned to your feelings as he talks about things that are disturbing. You must pull yourself back if you notice yourself shying away from your task of listening.

When you find yourself shying away from the task of listening, you are probably experiencing a feeling that is hard to tolerate. There's a good chance that this is also a feeling that is hard for your loved one to deal with. Hence, figuring out what you are reacting to may give you some insight into what your loved one is trying to avoid.

If you're having difficulty maintaining *your* end of the emotional experience, try doing the following after your discussion:

- Write down a list of the major feelings that you understand your loved one to be experiencing. Go over the list with someone else who knows what your loved one is going through. (That might be the trauma survivor himself.)

- Ask whether your list of his feelings is complete. If you've left out some significant feeling, it is likely to be a feeling that you aren't comfortable experiencing yourself and therefore have difficulty even perceiving when someone else is feeling it. It's likely to be rage, guilt, grief, or intense helplessness. Think about it: How often do you let yourself express that particular feeling?

- If your list is complete, you may not have a particular feeling that you've blocked. But for each feeling on the list, ask yourself how much you let yourself experience it.

- Think about how you felt when your loved one expressed each of those feelings. Were there particular points where you lost your concentration or distanced yourself from the feelings?

- Once you've identified your own emotional blocks, you can make a decision to overcome them. But even before you overcome them, your knowledge of them can help you become a better listener since you know what your blind spots are. Be on the lookout, and watch for those points in the conversation.

- You may have to let your loved one know that you have difficulty with certain feelings. This way he'll understand that the problem is not with him or what he's saying.

- Dealing with your own emotional blocks usually means uncovering feelings that you have buried. That requires you to talk to someone yourself! (It may or may not be the trauma survivor.)

- If you have no one with whom you can talk, or if you find that your blocks seem impenetrable, find a psychotherapist. You may do so individually, or you may want to see a family or couples therapist with your traumatized loved one. But take it one step at a time; you don't have to settle all these things ahead of time.

5. Talk About the Feelings as Separate Experiences

What is it like to feel terror, rage, extreme grief? As these overwhelming emotions are identified, they need to be examined from every possible angle. Distinct physical sensations are associated with every emotion, and each person's *physical* experience of their emotions is different. Stop and think for a moment about what it's like to *feel* fear. Some people sweat, others feel "butterflies" take flight in their stomachs. Then there are those whose temples throb in fright, and others whose voices suddenly go up an octave. Yet all of these physical reactions are ways of feeling the same emotion.

Every emotion involves not only physical reactions but specific thoughts and visual images. These too are different for each person. Since you want to learn what your loved one's exact experiences were and are, ask her to convey what it's like for her to experience the emotions she's identifying. You may ask not only "What was it like to be shot at?" but "What is it like to feel fear?" or "How do you know when you're afraid?" or "What happens when you're scared like that?'' These questions focus on the *feeling*—independent of the particular experience.

For example, you might say something like: "That sounds so frightening, I would have been scared to death. I don't think I've ever been that scared. What's it like to feel that scared? Were you aware of how scared you were right then, or did it catch up with you later? When I get scared, I feel it in my stomach. Where do you feel it? How do you know that you're afraid?" or "You said you were enraged. What did that feel like? Does your body feel a certain way when you get that angry? What thoughts go through your mind when you're in a rage like that? What sensations go through your body? Does it scare you to feel that intensely angry?"

6. Learn When to Back Off

I've encouraged you to help your loved one to delve into his traumatic emotions. This is a terrifying experience for him, and it may be for you as well. Now I must reverse myself and remind you that the reason he has buried these emotions in the first place is because they are overwhelming. That means that reexperiencing them can overburden his psychic capacity to function. He's likely to feel like he can't tolerate it if he's pushed too far or gets too carried away with his emotional reexperience of the trauma.

You must be prepared to help him back away if he feels he's gone too far. I recommend that you make your loved one your partner in evaluating whether he feels he's getting in over his head. If you think he's feeling overwhelmed and not talking about it, ask him. But if you find yourself asking frequently, it may be a sign that you're not reading him well or that you're expressing your own fear of his intense emotions.

Your goal is to help your loved one feel that he has some choice about how much he will let himself experience those frightening feelings. He needs to know that you're encouraging him to express them but that you will back off if he needs you to do so. You might say something like: "I want you to

talk to me about these things, but I understand that sometimes it's too much and you feel you can't talk about it. If I'm
pushing too much and you have to slow down, tell me. Let
me know if you feel you're getting in too deep. I believe we
can go further than you may think, but I'll back off if you let
me know that you need to stop. I don't think we have to leave
anything untalked about, but I certainly don't feel that it all
has to be done today. If you feel too overwhelmed, we can
come back to it later."

If the two of you agree that he's gone far enough and you
wish to help him stop for now, you can do so by switching
from *feeling* questions to *thinking* questions. You can bring
him back to the here and now by focusing on the actual discussion you're engaged in. This reduces the intensity of your
loved one's memories without leaving them altogether. It
also gives you the opportunity to continue if the two of you
feel up to it.

To turn the conversation from feeling to thinking, you
might ask questions such as these: "I can see that you're
getting really upset. Was it anything that I said? How would
you prefer I ask something like that? Do you think we were
pushing too hard, or did you just get surprised by some forgotten feeling? Is this what happened the other times you
tried to talk about the trauma? Do you want to take a break
here?"

If your loved one does enter the realm of feeling that he
has worked to avoid, he will *feel* overwhelmed. He may experience intense feelings of fear, sadness, anger, guilt, or other
emotions. He may sob uncontrollably—the scary part is the
uncontrollable aspect. He may think he's having a breakdown when he's seized by the intensity of these feelings, but
he's *not* having a mental breakdown. He's only experiencing
a depth of feeling that is so intense that it has a life of its own.
It won't last forever—in fact, it will last a few hours at most
and often only for a few minutes.

After this kind of emotional experience (called an abre-
action), your loved one will probably feel drained. He may
feel a lightness, as if he's finally relinquished a great burden.

He may feel vulnerable for days afterward. You should not let him feel forgotten during that period. Check in often, and make sure he's doing all right.

7. *What Meaning Has Your Loved One Given the Traumatization?*

Human beings cope with existence in a manner that is different from other forms of life. We think. We deal with life's events by creating meaning. One of the primary ill effects of traumatization is that the meaning we have created for our life is thrown askew. We lose our sense of certainty about ourselves. We come to doubt many of the things we believed before. Even our core beliefs—such as the purpose of life—can become meaningless. In its worst forms, traumatization can destroy the meaning of life! And without some kind of meaning, it's nearly impossible to go on.

An important part of the process of talking with your loved one is to help her straighten out this meaning dilemma. This can sound overwhelming when you consider the scope of your task. Most of us are not philosophers or theologians, and we don't really know what our own answers to such weighty questions are. But stop and think for a moment. The fact is that every one of us has found our own answers to these questions. The meaning you create for your personal life is expressed in your notions about who you are, what kind of person you are, and what kind of person you want to be.

You can help your loved one find her own answers to these questions. It's not as difficult as it sounds. Remember, she had answers before she was traumatized. Her objective is not to create meaning from scratch but to reconnect with the meanings she had, then make adjustments in those old answers that allow her to understand the changes she's been through. How can you help her make sense of those changes? Ultimately, she'll come up with the new answers herself, but she needs a forum—a sounding board—as the opportunity for her to examine herself and consider the changes she's undergone.

PTSD experts have identified basic questions that the trauma survivor must answer in order to make sense of it all. The following five questions, based on Dr. Charles Figley's model, provide a foundation for the process of reestablishing meaning in the survivor's life.

1. The survivor needs to consider *what happened* and to be able to make some sense of why it happened. He does this by talking to you about it. Everyone seeks to understand why terrible things happen.

2. The survivor must consider *why it happened to him*. He may have an explanation for why events occur as they do, but why did this one happen to him and not someone else? Why were some people hurt more than others? Why did something worse happen to someone else than to him?

3. *Why did he behave as he did* at the time? Trauma survivors are the ultimate Monday-morning quarterbacks. They review their actions over and over, pondering why they did this instead of that.

4. *How has he changed* as a result of the traumatization? He must look at himself, at what he was and at what he's become. You can help him take an objective appraisal of himself; your perspective can be invaluable.

5. The last question is similar to the third. Every trauma survivor thinks about *what he will do if it happens again*. He may not talk about it, but he thinks about it. It's another way he is trying to master the experience, so that next time he will be prepared.

These questions can provide a framework for you and your loved one to probe into the meanings of the traumatization. They aren't the whole agenda of your discussions, but they are issues that are likely to emerge if you're talking with her about her traumatization.

It's also important to talk with her about the losses she's experienced. Many survivors can't let go of their preoccupation with their trauma until they've mourned their losses. It's sometimes hardest to mourn the intangible losses—such as her innocence, her faith, or her sense of security—because it's hard to identify those losses. You can help her recognize the many things she's lost by talking about the loss of both tangibles and intangibles. Here are some other questions you might ask over the course of your discussions:

- How do you explain what happened?

- How do you think this experience has changed you?

- Where was your life headed before the trauma? Where is it headed now?

- Have you changed your attitudes and beliefs? What kind of world do you feel this is? How is that different from the way you used to perceive the world?

- What kinds of changes have taken place in your core beliefs, such as your beliefs about God, good and evil, justice, how the world works, right and wrong, what we should do with criminals, who deserves the breaks, and your purpose in life?

Contending with the Trauma Survivor's Symptoms

Talking with your loved one about his traumatization is even more difficult when he has symptoms. Many symptoms serve to keep him and you away from the emotionally loaded things that he should talk about. Sometimes the challenge for you is to hang in there and relate to him despite his symptoms. Many family members give up on trying to talk when their loved one is likely to get drunk, go into a rage, or withdraw from them. You must find a way to stay connected to your loved one despite his symptoms.

Here are some of the symptoms that you'll likely encounter.

Emotional Numbing

The most common symptom you'll encounter is emotional numbing. It's a tricky symptom because you're not always aware that it's going on. It can allow your loved one to discuss the trauma in such unemotional tones that she may be able to convince both you and herself that there's no underlying emotional issue that needs to be talked about.

Though I'm calling numbing a symptom here, as you'll recall, it's actually a coping mechanism. It allows her to function in a survival situation in which she might otherwise be paralyzed by intense emotions. But numbing becomes less a coping mechanism and more of a symptom as time goes by and she continues to bottle up any experience of intense emotion—or unloads all the emotion under one disguise, such as rage.

If your loved one shows little or no feeling about some part of her traumatization, don't assume that her feelings about it are resolved. You may have to try to get her to talk with you about it dozens of times before she finally begins to overcome her emotional blocks. You may be approaching the subject from many different directions or from the same direction, but as long as she continues to show emotional numbing all has not been said.

The hardest work for you may be dealing with the emotional numbing that you encounter in *other* areas of your relationship with your loved one. Numbing can be very difficult to tolerate when your spouse appears insensitive to your children or yourself. Trauma survivors who are entrenched in emotional numbing often seem cold, self-centered, cynical, and distant. They may make painful jokes about subjects that are not funny to you.

People who are exposed to high levels of human tragedy —emergency room workers, paramedics, policemen, firemen—often resort to morbid humor as a means of coping with tragedy. Among professionals who have devoted their lives to dealing with others' tragedies, this humor isn't an indication that they don't care; it's a way of numbing the pain so that they can continue to be around tragedy. Similarly, your loved one's cavalier attitude does not mean that she doesn't care. She's employing her emotional numbing because the feelings the situation evokes in her are too close to her feelings from the trauma. You need to understand that her caring is there; it's only that it's buried beneath a placid surface.

Elizabeth, the nurse in Vietnam who saw hundreds of young men die in her care, developed a stony exterior that revealed little emotion. She never cried and had a cynical attitude that her husband found exasperating. She almost never laughed with real humor. Instead, her laughter was a comment on the dismal nature of the world around her.

Only after years of therapy could she begin to show some of the enormous pain she felt about seeing so much death and human misery. She didn't know how to share these feelings with her husband. She viewed his concern about the little details of daily living as evidence that he was a superficial person and could never understand the depth of her pain. But as she began to share tiny bits of her painful experiences with him, she was surprised to discover that he was interested and supported her in her healing rituals, such as her pilgrimages to the veterans' memorial in Washington. The more she let him see the feelings underneath her stony exterior, the more understanding he became. She began to see that he had only seemed shallow because she had hidden her feelings and given him nothing to respond to that provoked emotions.

Difficulties with Closeness

All trauma survivors manifest difficulty with closeness. It's less severe for some, but it's agonizingly difficult for most. What can you do about it? How can you get past this problem in order to accomplish the task of talking? There are no simple answers to these questions. This difficulty with closeness is one of the very last symptoms to go in the healing process. In the meantime, the trauma survivor may see you as an intruder, an outsider, someone who is not wanted but is unfortunately needed. It's a lousy situation for you.

It helps to understand the origin of his difficulty with closeness. He sees an attachment as a potential place where he can get hurt, so he shies away easily. And he no longer knows himself. He's become a stranger to himself. This interferes with getting close to you or anyone. Put yourself in your loved one's shoes. It's hard to know who you love if you don't know who you are. You find yourself questioning your feelings, uncertain about how deep they go or whether they're even valid.

If a survivor was emotionally involved with someone before the trauma, he may feel that he was another person when he developed that relationship. He may not feel that he has much in common now with who he was, and perhaps he doesn't love the same kind of person. He may fear that he's not capable of loving anyone anymore, and he's fearful of losing anyone that he does love. But as he begins to feel more like himself again, many of those questions subside.

Rage Attacks

It is disconcerting, to say the least, to be the object of your loved one's rage when you're clearly working so much harder than anyone else to understand and support him. But trauma survivors—as well as people in general—often can't tolerate behavior in their loved ones that doesn't bother them in strangers. No one can get to you as much as the people who are important to you. You expect your loved ones to know how you wish to be treated, and when they fail you, you experience great disappointment. For many trauma survivors, that disappointment quickly leads to rage.

How can you deal with your loved one's rage attacks?

- First of all, don't provoke him. Remember that he's struggling to control his temper, despite appearances to the contrary.

- If he's becoming enraged, don't argue with him. Bring the discussion to a halt without trying to make your point one last time. Let him have the last word.

- Don't get defensive. Make an effort to listen and understand, even if you're not being listened to yourself.

- Try not to put him in a no-win situation. Leave him an out, a way to save face.

- If you do something that makes him feel helpless, he'll be closer to losing control. Try to help him feel some control. For example, let him decide what he would like to do now.

- If he starts to escalate, back off and stay away until he's calmed *himself* down. Remain calm yourself.

- Don't try to calm him down by talking to him like a child.

If your husband is a combat veteran, take this advice seriously. If he's subject to rage attacks, the worse thing you can do would be to fight back. I'm not advocating that you give in. I'm simply saying that you should "break contact" until he's in a better frame of mind. He's probably afraid of becoming violent himself. It will frighten him even more if he feels that you don't take seriously the possibility of his losing control. And if he gets scared, he's more likely to lose control. He'll be reassured if he knows that you respect the danger of provoking him and know when to break contact.

Nelson, a Vietnam combat veteran, had the ghastly experience of firing a machine gun into a hut that turned out to contain women and children. He was haunted by memories of this experience. After the war, he married and had children of his own. He thought he had put his war experience behind him, but when his children reached the age near that of those he had killed, he found it impossible to be close to them. He began to think more about that one afternoon in Vietnam—everything reminded him of it. He became increasingly distant from his family, sitting in front of the television for hours, speaking to no one.

When his wife tried to approach him to find out what was wrong, he'd get angry and insist she leave him alone. Several times she persisted, and he blew up—punching holes in the walls of their home, throwing things, and speeding off in his car. He would go to a bar and drink until he was so inebriated that he could return home without fear of blowing up again. What his wife didn't understand was that he left because of his fear of hurting her or the children. He was using the television and the alcohol to drown his painful memories and to stay away from the current reminders—his wife and children.

Social Withdrawal

Your loved one's withdrawal from the rest of society reflects her feeling about herself as different, and this is the area where she feels most changed by the trauma. It's painful to be around other people because that difference seems so much more apparent. She feels that she no longer belongs, that she's no longer part of the group, that she's an outsider. It's a very disheartening feeling, and she can keep it to a minimum by avoiding other people as much as possible.

Many activities can lead to an even greater sense of isolation on the part of the trauma survivor. For example, it's hard to be around ordinary people having fun because she's keenly aware that her life doesn't feel anything like fun. Depressed people have a hard time being around others who are obviously enjoying themselves, and of course, many trauma survivors are significantly depressed. It can be particularly difficult to be around a group of people enjoying something that she especially used to love. For instance, going to a softball game with her old team could be very difficult for a woman who used to really enjoy playing softball. Being there could heighten her awareness of how much she's changed and how she's no longer the same fun-loving person she used to be. Thus, she learns to avoid social situations in order to protect herself from feeling painfully different.

Another social scene that's particularly difficult for many trauma survivors is being around people who are caught up in something that the survivor regards as trivial. The survivor carries her tragedy around inside her head, and when she sees others intensely involved in something that appears unimportant to her, she's acutely aware of the disparity between her internal tragedy and the seemingly superficial concerns of others. She's apt to respond with anger, cynicism, or depression.

Consider what this is like for her. Suppose you've just left a room where a loved one is dying, and you encounter someone who's upset because her favorite soap opera has been preempted by a special news broadcast. You're not likely to have much sympathy for that person. If you live this way daily—always feeling as if you had just left a dying loved one—and you seem to continually encounter people upset over trivial things, you're quite likely to find yourself becoming angry and cynical. Your feelings of being different from others will increase, and you'll probably become more depressed. You'll stop caring about whether you're involved with others, not only because it's painful to feel so different but because you come to regard others as superficial and not worth the bother.

George and Frances are the parents of a little boy who was sexually molested by his teacher at preschool. The molestations were accompanied by physical threats. The entire family was traumatized by the experience, which took place over an extended period of time. For several months afterward, friends were understanding and interested, and the couple continued a variety of social contacts. But as time passed, they began to see less and less of their old friends. They felt that their friends were uncomfortable in their presence, and they found their friends' interests to be shallow compared to their ordeal. Their child was in therapy, and as the treatment progressed, new horrors were revealed. George and Frances talked less and less about it with the old friends and more with each other and with a network of new friends who had lived through similar events. As they found it increasingly painful to be around the old friends, their social lives made a permanent shift.

The issue of social alienation has a great impact on the loved ones of trauma survivors. As the survivor becomes more alienated, you feel a direct pull to become less involved yourself. If you pursue your own social activities with other people, you find that it increases the distance between you and your loved one. If you stay home with him, however, you become depressed and resentful, and he feels guilty. Eventually you fight. In either case, you come to feel more and more of that sense of being different yourself.

So what can you do? To begin with, respect the depth of his feeling of being different. Don't attempt to persuade or force him to enter into activities that will unnecessarily remind him of that difference. On the other hand, don't let him resign from the human race either. You can play a very important role in getting him out and involved. But you must carefully choose activities that he can tolerate as you slowly build toward more interactive pursuits. Some things to *avoid* include:

- large groups of strangers with whom he must interact (like a party with your co-workers);

- many of his old friends at once (rather than a few at a time, gradually);

- social activities in which he used to be highly involved and now shuns;

- activities that require high levels of audience participation (like playing charades); and

- activities for which he's not prepared (like surprise parties).

Instead, start with activities that are relatively undemanding. Go to the movies, out to dinner, or on a walk together. Go to public places together. See friends in small groups in which conversation can easily take place. When you're with special friends, help create an atmosphere in which feelings can be discussed. Don't let the conversation become overly superficial or tensely evasive of the trauma. People generally care and would like to be able to discuss it, but they often don't know whether to bring it up. Your loved one may be hesitant to talk about it as well. It's usually better if you don't talk about it for him; rather, encourage him to talk for himself. Support him when such conversations take place. Sit close to him. You're both still learning how to talk about these kinds of things—when to push on and when to back off. It's all right if he relies on your presence for a bit while he learns to talk with others about the difficult topics.

These are some of the things that you can do to help an adult who's been traumatized. In the next chapter, we'll discuss some of the special considerations involved when the trauma survivor is a child.

7

GUIDELINES FOR PARENTS
If the Survivor Is a Child

The most difficult trauma for any parent is the one that strikes their child. If you are such a parent, you're experiencing all the feelings you'd have for any other traumatized family member, with another dimension. Your feelings of responsibility and helplessness are enormous. You may be uncertain about the extent of your child's traumatization and how to interpret her behavior. And in the midst of taking care of her, you must take care of yourself. As you try to provide the right kind of response you fight your inclination either to deny or to overreact to the crisis. After a while, you may come to feel that you're scrutinizing your child and creating problems where none exist. If you and your spouse have different perceptions about the degree to which your child is affected, this creates additional family tensions.

A child's reaction to trauma doesn't always manifest itself in the same way it does with adults. Nor are they free to indulge in the same coping behaviors as adults. Indeed, many children manifest their psychological distress so differently from adults that it can easily go unnoticed. For example, they often develop sleep-related problems; they can't go to sleep, they wake up frequently, they become especially fearful at night, or they have bad dreams. Most children also regress in their physical and emotional development. They may have greater difficulty controlling their bladder or bowels, often redeveloping a problem (such as bed-wetting or thumb-sucking) that they'd previously outgrown. They frequently develop separation anxiety and find it very difficult to tolerate being away from their parents. Often, they start wanting to sleep with their parents again. And they may develop entirely new symptoms, particularly phobias in which they become highly fearful about some specific situation.

The traumatization of a child produces a trauma response that involves the entire family. From the outset, you yourself are traumatized because your ability to relate to your child's trauma is so extreme that you feel as though it happened to you. Dealing with this is complicated. You must provide the best possible environment for the recovery of the entire family, while maintaining a constant grasp of what your child needs. The guidelines for dealing with adult trauma are a beginning, but there are other factors that must be addressed when a child has been traumatized. Let us consider some of the ways in which children differ from adults and how these differences affect their reaction to trauma.

How Children Differ from Adults

Children are amazing creatures, both more fragile and more resilient than adults. They tend to express their feelings without inhibition; if a child likes you, he makes no secret of it, and if he doesn't like you, that's also readily apparent. Yet there are situations in which a child's feelings are less apparent, such as when there is conflict between his parents and the child is uncertain about his loyalties. When a child is uncertain about right and wrong—particularly in regard to his own behavior—he's prone to inhibit his feelings more.

And when a child has been traumatized, he may become inhibited about the expression of feelings related to the trauma. Yet children, like adults, need to explore and examine those feelings in order to come to terms with a traumatic experience.

Developmental Level

The first factor to consider with a traumatized child is his developmental level. Psychologists break child development up into many components such as language development, moral development, physical development, intellectual development, emotional development, and social development. Any of these areas can be relevant to a child's traumatization. The child's language development certainly bears upon his ability to talk about the trauma, while his intellectual development affects his ability to make sense of the experience. And the child's moral development affects his view of himself and others in regard to the trauma, as does his physical, social, and emotional development.

You may worry that you don't have enough expertise to assess your child's development, but I've found that most parents have a solid grasp of where their children are developmentally. You may not have a vocabulary of psychological labels, but you probably know what kinds of things your child can and cannot yet do. If you have questions about where your child is developmentally, you should consult a child psychologist or child psychiatrist.

Even if you feel confident in your understanding of your child, I recommend you make at least one visit to a professional. Even if all is going well, it won't be a waste of time because it's an opportunity for you to compare your impressions with those of the professional and to develop a relationship with someone upon whom you can call if the need arises.

A child's development changes rapidly, and one consequence of this is that new developmental stages often bring

renewed experience of the trauma. In effect, the child re-
works his resolution of the traumatization as he enters new
developmental levels and views it from different perspectives. For example, the meaning of a trauma is different to a
child at different levels of intellectual development as it is
influenced by his ability to generalize and conceptualize
dangers.

A Heightened Sense of Vulnerability

Preschool children are enormously dependent upon others to take care of them and consequently are subject to feelings of the most extreme vulnerability. Most adults are
protected from these raw feelings by their many skills for
dealing with the world, as well as by their illusions of security. But young children are still in the process of developing
these skills and manufacturing these illusions. Thus, they can
be thrust into the deeper feelings of vulnerability very
quickly.

Children protect themselves from vulnerable feelings using different means from adults. They place greater reliance
upon mechanisms like fantasy. Comic book and video
superheroes, for example, are extensions of children's fantasies. These superheroes are always endowed with powers
that allow them to overcome their vulnerabilities. Indeed,
superheroes are often portrayed as trauma survivors themselves, usually having been traumatized when they were children. Superman's home planet was exploded and his parents
killed; Batman's parents were killed by a criminal. Rather
than being overwhelmed by their vulnerability, these
superheroes developed abilities and powers that enabled
them to help others stricken by trauma.

Equally interesting is the fact that virtually all superheroes have secret identities and hide their powers from the
world. This allows a child to relate to the fantasy that he may
appear vulnerable on the outside but secretly he's invulnerable and therefore not really affected by the threats and

stresses of a hostile world. These fantasies may appear superficial to adults, but they are amazingly powerful in helping children cope with life.

Not only is the traumatized child upset by what happened and fearful of it happening again, he's now acutely aware of how vulnerable he is in regard to any number of dangers—not just the same one as the trauma involved. And not only must he come to terms with the specific trauma that he endured, he must find new ways of convincing himself that he's safe in general. In the meantime, he'll likely regress to an earlier developmental level, be more fearful, and be more in need of his parents' physical presence.

Part of the process of reachieving a feeling of security will be the resurrection of fantasies and illusions of security, such as in the superhero play referred to in Chapter 1. Your child's play will involve considerable fantasy and replaying of the trauma from many different perspectives. This is a healthy process in which she learns to master her fears.

If your child seems to be stuck on replaying the same situation over and over (for more than a few weeks), she may be having trouble finding ways to overcome the conflict that's expressed in the play. That can be a signal that she needs the help of a therapist, especially if she has other symptoms such as bed-wetting, tantrums, or other outbursts, refusal to separate from the mother, or a regression from levels of development that she had attained before the trauma. But the child who repetitively replays the trauma is less worrisome to me than the child who is so constricted and shut down by her traumatization that she cannot engage in even that spontaneous process. Those children should definitely receive therapy.

Alice, as a four-year-old, was molested by her parents' housekeeper's twelve-year-old nephew. The molestation consisted of the boy exposing himself and making Alice take off her pants. He told her not to tell, but Alice didn't like what happened and told her mother. Both parents talked with Alice about it. Although she was upset, she was open about it and seemed to accept that she was safe. But within a few weeks, she was found pretending to have a penis and to be showing it to another child. It came up in her play frequently after that.

Her parents contacted a therapist. The therapist saw Alice for a couple of sessions but concluded that Alice was simply working on what had happened by bringing it into her play. She had no other symptoms and seemed to have put the episode into a category of bad things that happened but did no permanent damage. The therapist counseled the parents about how to respond to Alice's play and stayed in touch with them over the following year. Alice did fine; she had several talks with her mother about the event, then lost interest in it and it disappeared from her play.

Capacity to Forget

Children do not forget the same way adults do. Their minds are soaking up information at a much higher rate, and they don't possess the psychological mechanism that allows adults to simply forget things that are too disturbing. This mechanism, called *repression*, is an unconscious process that apparently becomes available to children in the early years of elementary school. Before that, children cannot avoid overly disturbing thoughts and feelings by repressing them, so they must employ a different mechanism. Children under six primarily rely upon a process called *dissociation*, in which they replace the disturbing thought with something different. This replacement process is quite far-reaching. It's not simply that the one thought is replaced by another; rather, the child's entire state of mind is shifted.

The traumatized child uses dissociation to shift from feeling small and vulnerable to a state where he can feel more powerful and invulnerable. All children use dissociation, though the content of their fantasies varies. Some children dissociate to a pleasant place where there are no dangers, while others dissociate to a world of secret powers. Dissociation is worrisome when the child begins to think of himself as a different person altogether, in order to feel that the bad things are happening to *someone else*. Children in situations of severe, ongoing abuse frequently resort to dissociating right out of their personality. In order to avoid the terrible thoughts and feelings associated with abuse, the child develops alternative personalities (multiple personality disorder) to which to escape.

If you believe your child is dissociating, please don't let my reference to alternative personalities frighten you. Again, dissociation is a normal phenomenon in which *all* children engage and an important aspect of how they cope with trauma. Children dissociate to some degree whenever they engage in fantasy, a major form of their play. Every time your child pretends, she is dissociating to some extent. By four to five years old, children know the difference between their pretend world and the real world. If you fear your child has lost that awareness or is not behaving like herself, consult a professional.

Rachel was a teenager when she ended up in residential treatment for her psychological problems. When she was younger, her parents were physically abusive of her, punishing her with severe spankings and locking her in closets. When she was older, they tried to control every aspect of her life. Yet Rachel went around with a little smile on her face and never complained. She had learned to "go to other places" when she didn't like what was happening around her. After her experience with her cruel parents, she never got very close to people and couldn't trust anyone. As a young child forced to sit in the dark in a cramped closet, she'd become adept at imagining herself in different circumstances. It required many years of intensive treatment for her to give up her fantasy world and risk letting her life be real again.

Rachel is an example of an unhealthy extreme reliance on dissociating. It was her primary means of coping with her situation and became a way of life for her. That's partly because her trauma was of the recurring variety; she learned to expect it and to anticipate it by being off in her "other place." Most children dissociate as part of dealing with their traumatization; indeed, it's an important element in children's use of fantasy. We're only concerned when it goes awry.

Importance of Parents

The parents' importance in maintaining a child's psychological balance cannot be overemphasized. A child doesn't possess the skills, knowledge, experience, or strong ego to cope with life's daily difficulties—much less the exceptional ones required by traumatization. But nature has provided a way for her to survive, even flourish, despite life's inevitable frustrations and disappointments—you. Before she develops her own strong ego to guide and support her, she can rely upon your ego.

When I refer to the *ego*, I'm talking about that part of us that is responsible for learning to deal with our environment —for planning our actions and managing our internal emotional tides. Adults are able to calm themselves when they get overwrought, discipline themselves when they would like to act impulsively, and maintain an appreciation for who they are and how they see themselves fitting into the larger scheme of things. Your child is unable to do these things for herself; she must rely upon you. She's particularly dependent upon your ego to help her deal with traumatic situations. She can weather the storm if she continues to have access to a strong, reliable parent who provides the stability and security that she's unable to provide herself.

The preschool child's secondary trauma is embedded in his relationship with his parents. His experience of a secondary trauma is essentially determined by you—your attitudes about him, your ability to mediate between him and the greater social world, and your personal well-being and capacity to deal with the trauma. If your view of him changes, his view of himself will suffer. If your relationships with your social world change or if you interfere with his opportunities to develop a social world, he may suffer the effects of a secondary trauma.

The younger he is, the more your child depends on your ego functioning to maintain his own. If your ego falls apart or if you stop providing support for him, it's as if he were directly traumatized once again. If your child is traumatized and *you* can't deal with it, he'll be unlikely to be able to deal with it either. That's why it's essential that you take proper care of *yourself*, so that you can be stable for your child. He bases his sense of security on his reading of you and your confidence. If you find that you're unable to provide that stability, get professional help for yourself so that you can do your job for your child.

Of course, one of the worst traumas a child can experience is to have something happen to his parent. The child's sense of himself as an individual is still poorly developed and very dependent upon his parents. In this culture, children don't achieve much emotional separateness until the latter stages of elementary school. They remain physically dependent upon their parents through adolescence, and many are financially dependent upon their parents well into adulthood. Throughout all these stages, the loss of a parent causes a profound disruption in the child's sense of self.

The Impact of Separation

Since you play such a vital role in helping your traumatized child feel secure, separations from you are extremely difficult for your child. Children in early grammar school may cling like two-year-olds again. Your child becomes more aware of her vulnerability and depends more explicitly upon you. Parting from you comes to represent a sudden exposure to all the dangers at once, and a moment of separation can become a crisis of major proportions. You may have difficulty understanding the depth of her fear at that moment, especially if the separation is to be brief (such as going out to the car to bring in the groceries).

This separation anxiety may be played out differently by different children, but it's an issue for all traumatized children. It often comes up at bedtime. Bedtime can become a major battlefield because sleep can come to represent the state of total vulnerability that she associates with your absence.

Many traumatized children return to the familiar sleep routines they learned when they were younger, such as holding stuffed animals, saying their prayers, or having their parents read to them. But they may lack such familiar routines to deal with waking up in the middle of the night with nightmares or night terrors. Many traumatized children want to sleep with the parents again because they are too afraid to sleep alone. Parents often give in to this request, because battling over sleeping arrangements can be too great a hassle. You may have found it necessary to do this, but you should work toward helping your child regain her ability to sleep alone. If sleeping with you becomes the new norm, you'll be faced with an additional problem in the future.

One way or another, your child is likely to regress in dealing with separation from you—whether by having sleep problems, avoiding school, or just refusing to let you out of her sight. You must respond to her increased separation anxiety by recognizing the fear and not requiring her to do more than she can handle, though it's often not easy to know how much that really is. Your goal is to help her return to the level of competence she'd acquired before the trauma, so that she can resume her developmental path. It's a mistake to allow her to regress—such as resuming the habit of sleeping with you—then accept this behavior as the new status quo. If you communicate acceptance that the regressed behavior is now the norm, it can interfere with her development.

Knowing how fast and how hard to push her to resume greater levels of competence is tricky, however. But no one knows a child as well as her parents do. You know when her tears indicate terror and when they're more of a manipulation. You're a good judge of how quickly she's able to tolerate separations. And you can facilitate her progress both by encouraging her and by setting appropriate limits on the regressed behavior.

Importance of Peers

As your child gets older, his dependence upon you changes. It will be a long time before he truly abandons his reliance upon you, but as he matures, other people join you in their importance to him. This change is reflected in his fears. Up until elementary school, his primary concern tends to be that something physical might happen to him or to you. But around age six, he begins to worry about more social kinds of issues, involving how others view him. As he advances through grammar school, he worries about being ridiculed by his peers or not performing well in school or athletics. By the time he reaches adolescence, fears about being different are a major factor in how he makes decisions. The meaning of a trauma, too, changes with his age. For a young child, a disfiguring accident is a brush with death; for an adolescent, it is rather the "kiss of death" because it makes him different and more likely to be rejected by his peers.

The shift here is from physical to social concerns. A child who was traumatized when younger may reconsider the trauma and have to rework his resolution of it as he grows older. It becomes a new trauma as he focuses on how it makes him different from other kids. He may become symptomatic again—or for the first time—as he struggles with the newly discovered implications of what happened to him. And as he approaches adolescence, he's less able to rely upon the stability of his parents' egos in order to cope. He must come to terms with the trauma more on his own. Even if he does regress and allows his parents to determine how he deals with it internally, he'll eventually have to come to a personal resolution. Otherwise, he'll remain dependent upon them and gain no confidence in his ability to deal with life.

Children aren't born with defenses; defenses develop as

the child matures. Preschool children use immature defenses that aren't as sturdy as those of adults. Young children rely heavily upon denial—they simply insist that they're not experiencing a disturbing thought or feeling, or that a disturbing event hasn't occurred or doesn't bother them. For example, a child who's angry with her mother may yell "I'm not angry." Even though it's clear to her mother that she's angry, she's not aware of it. In traumatic situations, the child may insist that she's not frightened or that the situation wasn't frightening. This style of protecting herself is all right, but there aren't a lot of backup defenses if denial proves inadequate.

Children's limitations in this area are revealed when we try to get them to talk to us about their traumatic experiences. Preschoolers don't have the ability to discuss the trauma dispassionately, which requires the defense mechanism of emotional numbing. Thus, in encouraging the child to recall the trauma, we can easily push her beyond her capacity to protect herself. When this happens, she may insist on not talking, say "No, no," or literally put up her hands and try to push away the distressing thought and physically protect herself from the assault of the questioning.

In Chapter 4, we saw that the development of meaning is an essential aspect of the recovery process. This is as true for children as it is for adults, but it's different for children. Their capacity to think abstractly develops very slowly, extending all the way into adolescence. Your child's explanations for the event might make no sense to you. Sometimes young children exhibit "magical thinking"—believing that thinking a thing makes it so. Your child may find a way to believe that the trauma can never re-occur because of convoluted reasons, such as insisting a burglar would not return because he was just "testing" the house for security.

Your child's process of finding meaning for her trauma will be different from your own. Sometimes she will follow the same logic as you; at other times she'll have her own logic. When she talks, you may be deceived into thinking that you understand the subject in the same way she does, only to discover later that she came away from the conversation with an entirely different meaning—one with which she may still be satisfied. Because they are different ages and at different developmental levels, children in the same family often form very different meanings and have very different reactions to the same trauma.

Pablo and Juanita had three sons, Manuel, age four, Raul, age seven, and Pablo, age nine. Pablo Senior committed suicide, and Juanita felt it was best to keep this from the boys. All the boys knew was that their father had died a violent death, but they were unclear on the details. Lacking a clear understanding about how their father died, each boy had his own story.

Although it was not acknowledged in the family that there had been a suicide, it is most likely that Juanita's feelings about the way her husband died affected the children's stories.

In therapy, the boys were each asked to draw a picture of what had happened to their father. The differences among the drawings were extreme, but they were quite instructive in revealing the way each boy explained this trauma. Pablo, the oldest boy, drew his father endangering himself in a foolhardy fashion. Raul drew his father being assassinated by an evil stranger, and Manuel drew an auto accident. In addition, each boy developed his unique reaction to the event: Pablo was depressed, Raul became a clown, and Manuel was angry.

I think Pablo somehow recognized that his father was responsible for his own death and so became depressed. Raul avoided any awareness of either his father's problems or his own feelings—by creating an evil stranger and hiding behind the mask of a clown. And Manuel, as the youngest, may not have appreciated his father's responsibility for his own death and felt freer than the others to express his anger about the loss.

The Use of Play

Parents are often distressed to discover that their child is playing out the trauma situation with other children. Children use play to examine, reexperience, and master traumatic events and to provide meaning for them. A child's interest in replaying out situations related to the trauma should not be squelched, though it may need to be *structured*. Depending upon the nature of the trauma, it is sometimes best to provide a protected setting for the child to do this play.

We'll discuss your response to your child's traumatic play at the end of this chapter. Some parents feel comfortable engaging in this play themselves, but others prefer to take their children to a professional therapist so that the majority of this playing can occur in the best possible environment. Here are some things that all parents should do if their children have been through a traumatic experience.

Guidelines for Helping Traumatized Children Recover

Make Them Feel Safe

Your first goal is to make your traumatized child feel safe again. You must help him feel that the traumatization is not going to recur. This may mean taking behavioral precautions and/or reassuring him of your awareness of and preparedness for the danger. Safety is his first concern—little progress will be made until he feels that the trauma is not going to recur. This may not mean anything more than speaking to him about his feeling unsafe, but he needs to know that you're tuned in. It also helps to reassure him that you will not ignore his perceptions of danger.

One night while Joey, a four-year-old boy, and his sister Maggie, a six-and-a-half-year-old girl, were at home with a babysitter, a small fire broke out in the kitchen that threatened to overtake the entire house. The babysitter handled the emergency well, first getting the children outside and then calling the fire department from a neighbor's house. The fire department came and put the fire out. The children also handled it well at the time by being obedient to the babysitter and remaining calm. But after several days, Joey began to express a great deal of interest in fires and how people come to die in them. He began to have sleep problems and obsessed about the many things that could happen to him when his parents were absent. Later, separations started to become major battles, and his mother contacted a therapist.

The therapist drew the family's attention to the fire and suggested it may have traumatized Joey. His parents immediately took a number of steps to deal with the boy's fear that another fire could occur, especially when they were out. They installed smoke detectors, placed several fire extinguishers in the house (including one in the kitchen), and practiced fire drills. The beauty of their effort was that they did it all as a family. Everyone came up with ideas, which included a family visit to the local fire station to meet the firemen.

Joey's symptoms cleared up very quickly. He personally dealt with the trauma in a number of ways, including playing with toy fire engines with his father and sister. His parents remained firm about separations. They acknowledged his fears but maintained that they had to be away at times and that they would always make sure he would be safe with someone while they were gone. But they took the possibility of fire very seriously, and they treated the issue as a family problem—not as simply their son's problem! I believe that because Joey felt his fears were taken very seriously and was reassured, he was able to relinquish his less realistic separation fears.

Reestablish Normalcy

One of the most important conditions that allows your child to function at her maximum potential is a consistent, predictable environment to live in. She requires consistency to be able to deal easily with her external environment, but it is also necessary for the internal contributions it makes to the development of her personality and the maintenance of her psychological health. She places particular importance on the image of herself that is reflected in the ways you deal with her. Your view of her has a formative influence on her character, and if that view falters, she will suffer.

Every traumatized child needs her own personal place to return to, where she can feel secure. Here she feels most herself and has the greatest chance of overcoming the effects of the traumatization. In order to help her recreate a safe place, you must communicate your positive view of her. You must communicate interest in hearing about the trauma and sympathy for the overwhelming emotions, but you must also communicate that life hasn't changed all that much, that she's still the same person and you expect her to live by the same standards as before the trauma. You might say something like: "Something terrible happened, but we love you just as much as ever, and you still have to take a bath and go to bed on time." This is one of the most reassuring messages your child can hear; now she can return to squabbling with you over bedtimes.

Hear the Fears, But Bedtime Is Still Bedtime

If your child doesn't feel secure, it may be necessary to make changes in the old routines. If your child was bitten by a stray dog, he may now refuse to go outside alone because he feels unsafe. Your only response here is to accompany him outside. It would be wrong to put him back into a situation where he genuinely feels unsafe—it doesn't build courage or character or anything like that. But if he generalizes his fear to include situations that are far afield of the unsafe one, he may be developing a different kind of problem. He may refuse to leave your side at all, even in the safety of home. Be clear in your response to him that you know what the danger is and will see to it that he is safe from it. Help him distinguish situations that have potential dangers from those that don't.

Most children react to trauma by becoming more dependent upon their mother again, so a mother's job is to accept the increased dependency and reassure the child that she is available. But her long-term goal is for the child to reattain separateness. She must take seriously the child's fears, and change some rules and routines while insisting that others remain the same. In the following example, the fears are accepted as reasonable. The parents explain what they've done to address the real danger, and they talk with their child about his fears, but they also communicate that his fears don't alter the basic needs of the family. If you're in a similar situation, you might try saying something like this:

"We're going to go out tonight and leave you here with Aunt Leslie and Uncle Jerry. We've talked with them about what happened when the man came into the house. The window he got in through is barred up now, and no one can get in through there or any of the other windows. Aunt Leslie and Uncle Jerry know that you're scared of being left alone again, and they won't leave you alone at all. One of them will be with you all the time. We're going to be at the Wilsons, and Aunt Leslie and Uncle Jerry have the phone number there. We'll be home by 10:00 and we expect you to be asleep by then."

If the child balks at being left with the relatives, you can question him: "Don't you feel safe with Aunt Leslie and Uncle Jerry? What do you think can happen? Would it help if you could talk to us? If you want, we can call just before your bedtime and talk to you then. I know you don't want us to go out, but Mommy and Daddy need to see their friends. We wouldn't go if we didn't know for sure that you would be safe with Aunt Leslie and Uncle Jerry. All the phone numbers are written down for you. Here's the police number, the next-door neighbor's, and here's the Wilsons', where we'll be.''

Don't Lose Sight of Your Healthy Child

For some parents, the most difficult part of dealing with their child's traumatization is retaining their view that the child is psychologically all right. If you see your child as damaged and irrevocably changed, you'll inevitably communicate this to him in the many subtle and nonsubtle ways we influence our children. And the more you communicate a view that he's permanently damaged, the more you'll hamper his confidence that he can overcome the blow. Even a physically impaired child must be seen as a whole person who resides in a damaged body. The child may be inevitably changed in ways that will restrict his future, but the soundness of his emotional life does not have to be permanently destroyed.

You and your spouse must help each other get past such fears so that you can provide the best possible environment for recovery. If your fears persist, you should seek professional help for yourselves. A fearful parent is not helping a fearful child; your child measures his confidence in himself by his perception of your confidence in him.

You can reassure him by telling him something like: "I know you're scared that it could happen again. But we've tried to make sure it won't. We know that what happened was terrible and that you're still scared. But you'll get over this thing, and you'll still be you. We still have you, and you still have us. We love you just as much as we ever did, and now that we know how this can happen, we'll do everything we can to see that it never does. It's very scary, but you're still okay.''

Maintain Your Own Emotional Stability

To a large degree, your child's sense of self depends upon your confident view of her, but her continued sense of security depends upon your confidence in yourself and your own stability. Your ability to remain calm in the face of emotionally distressing experiences provides a vital function for your child. In traumatic situations and their aftermath, she gauges her security by her perceptions of your confidence. Do you appear confident and in control of yourself, despite the frustrations and fears that the situation evokes? Or do you display considerable anxiety and feelings of helplessness and being overwhelmed? If you appear stable, in control, and not overly worried, your child is much more likely to feel secure and to reestablish her own confidence and competence in dealing with life.

Provide a Stable Recovery Environment

The first step toward providing the ideal recovery environment involves your image of your child. You must recognize that your child is not permanently damaged in the sense of being no longer able to deal effectively with life. You must communicate this recognition based on your actual belief that it is true. Come to terms with this! This belief alone will provide an emotionally stabilizing influence on your child in which he can begin to come to terms with what has happened to him. In addition, realizing that it is true can help stabilize *you.*

We all know stories of children and adults who successfully deal with the most terrible of physical disabilities. Every individual who manages to make such an enormous adjustment is able to do so because she still feels herself to be a whole person. The same holds true for recovery from severe emotional trauma. Your child's ability to hold on to his sense of himself as a whole person is primarily dependent upon his perception of your perceptions of him.

Your second step is to convey your own emotional stability to your child by remaining calm yourself. This doesn't mean that you're never upset or unsure. Nor does it mean that you should present an artificial "happy face" around your child that parodies your real feelings. Rather, it simply means that you should make an effort to be steady for your child when you're together. You can discuss his fears and your own assessment of the dangers that may exist, but the central issue is that you must not burden him with your own fears. For your own emotional support, you must go elsewhere. You can be close to your child, but, above all else, he shouldn't be made to feel he must reassure *you*. If you need to "fall apart," do so at a time and place to which your child won't have access. It's best if you have someone else to do this with. It will relieve your temptation to use your child as an emotional confidant. If you don't have a spouse, do everything possible to find adult emotional supports for yourself!

Be a Willing Audience

I recommend that you talk with your child about her traumatic experience. But you should realize that it will probably not go as it would with an adult. Your child may not be willing to talk about it in the setting or at the time your schedule dictates, nor in the same way. The timing and pacing will be largely determined by your child. She may not talk about it at all, but expresses it through other means, such as in art or play. You must be open to these alternative modes of "discussing" the trauma. You can ask about it, but don't force her to talk if she isn't ready. Instead, let her know you're a willing audience, and be prepared to stop and try to understand whenever she expresses something related to the trauma.

One of the frustrations of dealing with traumatized children is that they often cannot tell us what we feel we need to know. Some parents pressure their children to talk about the trauma. If you find yourself doing this, you should realize that it does more harm than good. Despite your own feelings of helplessness, you must respect your child's style of dealing with the trauma (even if it's nonverbal) and work with it, not against it. A child constantly questioned about the trauma is likely to feel that she's done something wrong and/or that she's still not safe.

If she's able to discuss it calmly, it's all right to ask her questions to make sure you know everything she can tell you about it. But, if you question her endlessly because you never feel that you know enough, she can come to feel persecuted. In any event, your child may *never* tell you everything you would like to know. Young children have a poor ability simply to recall events; their memories work better at *recognition* than at recall. That's why your kindergartener gives monosyllabic answers when you ask about her day. She really doesn't recall much about it. Yet later, she sings a new song or tells you detailed stories that give you an idea of how much she did learn. These memories aren't forgotten—they don't emerge until something stimulates them. She hasn't developed the adult's tricks of organizing memories so that they can be retrieved easily.

Help Your Child Sort Out the Feelings

It is helpful to know the facts. Unfortunately, many traumatized children cannot supply adults with adequate information. Children who have been abused are often sworn to secrecy and fear retribution or getting their abusers in trouble. If you were present during the trauma, your factual knowledge won't be a problem. But if you were absent, you can easily become obsessed with your need to know exactly what happened, particularly if the trauma was recurring.

What's more important, however, is to learn how your child felt and continues to feel about the incident. Probe gently by saying something like: "It can be very confusing to have something happen like you've been through. We often don't know how we really feel after something like that.

Some children would be scared, but others would be angry. How did it make you feel? Sometimes we feel one way at the time, and then we feel another way afterward. Do you remember how you felt at the time? What about now? How do you feel about what happened?"

Responding to the Traumatic Play

When your child expresses something trauma-related in his play, the best response you can make is to show that you recognize the message and to comment about the feelings involved. This is your opportunity to learn how he feels and help him sort it out for himself. For example, if a dog-bitten child draws a dog biting a boy, you may talk about his being scared, but you may discover that he also feels angry or guilty. You may not know what feelings he ascribes to the dog —was the dog angry or scared? The child often doesn't know himself and is looking to you for help.

The following approach would be helpful to the child: "Oh, that doll's hitting the other doll with the baseball bat. Does that mean he's angry? I guess that's why people hit other people. I wonder how the doll feels about being hit. She probably feels pretty bad. She probably doesn't understand why someone would hit her like that. Maybe she's angry too. Or maybe she's just afraid she'll get hit again. What do you think?"

You don't have to be a professional therapist to talk to your child about the feelings he's experiencing. It's very helpful for him just to have his feelings recognized and validated with words like: "You're scared, I would be too." *The most damaging feelings are those that are never discussed.* The child then lives alone with emotions that are overwhelming to him. If you're not certain what your child is feeling, ask about possible feelings, such as: "Maybe you're angry that we didn't prevent this from happening."

This chapter has focused on the child who's been traumatized directly. But as I indicated in Chapter 3, the effects of trauma touch all members of a family. Hence, even when the trauma occurred to an adult, the children are affected. Some of the things I've had to say in this chapter certainly hold true for that situation as well, particularly the need for the parents to maintain their own emotional stability for the children. But there's another whole level of recovery in which you can help your entire family, regardless of whether the survivor is a child, an adult, or the entire family. That level is when you do things *as a family* to deal with your trauma, which is the focus of Chapter 10. Dealing with a family member's traumatization as a family can bring the family together as they've never been before.

Part III

HEALING

8

OVERCOMING THE
PHYSICAL SYMPTOMS
Feeling Yourself Again

The more time has passed since the primary trauma occurred, the more the symptoms have become a way of life, so
much so that they may persist even if the trauma itself has
been resolved. These symptoms include: physical symptoms
associated with anxiety, depression, and hyperarousal;
symptoms of a damaged sense of self (problems controlling
rage and maintaining self-esteem); and interpersonal symptoms of distrust and an inability to maintain intimacy.

These problems must be worked on directly—they won't
necessarily improve when the primary trauma has been resolved. The resolution of the primary trauma sometimes
leads to an immediate reduction in these symptoms, but the
longer you've lived with the trauma, the more the symptoms
will have become part of your life.

Stress is the cause of many of these symptoms, and the
name Post-traumatic Stress Disorder implies that trauma

165

stresses the individual beyond normal limits. When you stop and examine the effects of excessive stress, the results are awesome. It is the cause of a huge number of physical illnesses, as well as the more obvious manifestations—headaches, muscular tension, and ulcers. Many people see cardiopulmonary fitness—via aerobic exercise—as the best defense against stress. Yet stress still affects even those people who are in the best physical condition. And if "ordinary" stress is so powerful, what must we conclude about the power of *traumatic stress*?

Stress

The stress caused by traumatization can be so severe that it would literally overwhelm people if they allowed themselves to experience it fully. When the traumatization involves a single event, it's virtually impossible to fully experience all the feelings evoked at that moment. Those feelings come back over time as the person recalls the event and relives it in her mind. So trauma survivors learn to rely upon mechanisms that allow them to dilute, contain, avoid, deny, forget, and otherwise remain distant from these feelings. Meanwhile, they experience stress.

Everyone lives with a certain amount of stress in their daily life. Current thinking is that although this is not necessarily a bad thing, it can contribute to problems if they don't deal with it constructively. It appears that each person has an optimal stress level, at which they are energized and challenged to perform at their maximum. But when a person goes over that optimal level, his performance falls and he begins to suffer physical consequences. There may be good stress and bad stress, but whatever way you look at it, traumatic stress is not good. If you're living with the stress of an unresolved trauma, most of your resistance to stress has been absorbed in your daily dealings with this hidden burden. Therefore, your tolerance for additional stress is low— you're already beyond your optimal level of stress before you even get out of bed in the morning!

Everyone reacts to excessive levels of stress in their own peculiar ways. Some people become sick a lot. Others get angry, or depressed, or fatigued. Still others get ulcers or heart attacks. It helps to figure out your own unique ways of reacting to stress. Then you can spot it more easily when you're stressed and try to take action sooner.

Tune In to Your Physical Experience

If you are a trauma survivor, many of your present symptoms can be traced back to your efforts to avoid feelings associated with the trauma. Many survivors begin to drink or work too much or withdraw socially because they are trying to stay away from the feelings associated with the trauma. Are you trying to avoid feeling a certain way? As you reflect on this, bear in mind that feelings are experienced as physical, bodily sensations. Different people experience similar feelings in different ways. One person knows he's fearful because he has butterflies in his stomach, while another feels his heart pounding, another gets a lump in his throat, and another gets watery legs.

How do you know when you're fearful? Or when you're anxious, angry, or excited? These feelings may increase your metabolism, elevating your blood pressure, heart rate, and muscle tension. Your breathing rate may also increase, and you're likely to consume more oxygen and produce adrenaline. These are all part of the fight-or-flight response, in which the body goes into a state of arousal to deal with whatever it is that the person is excited about. But if there's nothing to be done once you're geared for action and you maintain this aroused state for extended periods of time, you'll begin to stress your bodily resources.

By contrast, depression and sadness tend to be associated with *decreases* in heart rate and oxygen consumption. Indeed, severe depression slows down your reflexes, both mentally and physically. You're not as quick-witted, and you can't perform at your usual physical level. So whether you're experiencing an arousing feeling, such as fear, or a retarding feeling, such as depression, you come to identify the feeling in part by how you "feel" physically.

If you think about this physical aspect of feelings, you begin to understand why stress can produce physical illnesses, aches, and pains. Under stress, your muscles are tensing, your glands increase the production of certain hormones, and your body overtaxes systems designed to run at rest most of the time. If you are not aware of this inner turmoil you get a situation where the water is boiling over and nobody is watching the stove. Your immunity system is overtaxed but you don't recognize the need to do something about it.

So I recommend that you *tune in* to your physical experience and notice these physical changes. You might stop and consider right now: What muscles are you tensing? Try relaxing your shoulders. Do they droop? If so, you may have been tensing them unconsciously.

Learn to Breathe

Breathing is an amazingly important part of your ongoing state of tension versus relaxation. The natural rate, flow, volume, rhythm, and depth of breathing vary with the situation. It speeds up to deal with increased demands and stimulating emotions. When you relax, your breathing slows down and becomes less laborious; you breathe more shallowly and rapidly when you're in a stressed state, more slowly and deeply when you're relaxed and free of anxiety.

Becoming more aware of your breathing can help you relax and deal with your tension and stress more effectively. Breathing awareness is an essential part of meditation, which basically clears the mind while the body is relaxed. Using breathing techniques, you can just take a moment, relax, and slow down internally. You may also become more aware of how you sit, and notice when your posture is interfering with deeper breathing.

Pursue a Program of Stress Relief

Your most critical step here is to take seriously the need to relieve stress. Keep yourself in the best possible physical health: this means attending to your diet, getting enough exercise, sleep, rest, and free time, and controlling what goes into your body. You also need to keep yourself in the best possible *mental* health; this means maintaining relationships in which you feel sufficiently accepted to be emotional and discuss stressful events.

Decide what specific things you will do to relieve stress. It helps to have regular devices—such as daily exercise time—and optional devices—such as the breathing exercises—that you can employ as needed. Doing some kind of exercise is important, but don't pursue it to the degree that it feels like self-punishment. And think about the things that help you relax. You may get more relaxation and enjoyment out of listening to music or building birdhouses than out of doing aerobics.

Learn to recognize when you're stressed and need relief. To improve your awareness of your physical state, take a yoga class, or tai chi chuan, or transcendental meditation, or dance, or massage. Join a softball team. Do whatever you can lose yourself in as you focus on your physical experience. Becoming so engrossed in an activity that you "lose yourself" is probably a good indicator that you've found an effective form of relaxation. Some forms of relaxation, such as sports, are very active, while others, such as reading, are very quiet and slow. It's best to have both kinds in your repertoire. The wider the range of activities to which you can turn, the more resilient you will tend to become to daily stress.

Change Your Niche

In Chapter 4 we discussed how trauma survivors can become embedded in a niche that's not good for them. They may be pursuing stress relief in nonproductive ways. If you're still trying to recover from a traumatization that occurred quite a few years ago, the chances are that you've developed some unhealthy ways of coping. These "unhealthy" ways may work to some degree, but unhealthy coping usually creates new problems even as it deals with the old problems.

Turning to alcohol is an example. Many trauma survivors drink as a way of coping. It takes the edge off the intrusive traumatic memories, helps the person be more social and get to sleep at night, and generally makes life more bearable. But if the drinking goes too far, it creates a rash of new problems. The memories leak out anyway, and the person acts foolishly when drunk; new social problems develop, he wakes up in the middle of the night and can't get back to sleep, and life becomes a different kind of hell. Now alcohol has become the problem.

Obviously, alcohol is a problem for many people, not just people who have been traumatized. If you are abusing alcohol, you'll need help overcoming it—independent of dealing with your traumatization. A variety of professional programs are available to help you, but don't rule out Alcoholics Anonymous, one of the most powerful and effective sources of help. If you've been traumatized *and* are alcoholic, make sure you see a professional therapist who can help you juggle *both* these aspects of recovery. There are other drugs that people often abuse in their efforts to deal with stress—and not only illegal drugs. Many people abuse legal, nonprescription drugs, such as caffeine and nicotine.

Changing your niche means making the changes in your life-style that will allow you to live a healthier life. By *niche* I mean your external environment, as opposed to your psychological or internal environment. Changing your niche means developing new and different social relationships and doing different activities—in other words, new habits. Three guidelines can help you in your efforts to change your niche:

1. *Focus on your external environment.* If you're trying to stop drinking, don't hang out at the bar.

Move the liquor out of the house, and don't hang around with your drinking companions. Changing the external setting can make it easier to uphold your internal decisions.

2. *Replace bad habits with good habits.* Don't just stop what you've been doing; replace it with something better. Pursue an exercise program, take up a class in something of interest, or start a new project at home—these can focus your energies in a positive direction, rather than keep you trying *not* to focus them in a negative direction.

3. *Don't define slipping as failure.* Rather than promising yourself that you'll never return to the old habit, focus instead on always returning to the new habit, should you ever temporarily lose your way. Many people fail to develop a new habit because they approach it as if any regression to the old habit indicates failure. How many people have you known who tried to quit smoking, smoked one cigarette, then decided they'd "failed" and resumed smoking?

Sleep Problems

People with stress disorders have sleep problems for a variety of reasons, and they have to be approached in different ways. First, if you have sleep problems, you must identify what kind you have. Some people have difficulty falling asleep, while others have difficulty staying asleep or getting out of bed in the morning. Some awaken early and can't go back to sleep. (Most people with stress disorders don't have the problem of sleeping *too* much.) Different sleep problems stem from different causes; thus, a person can have more than one kind of sleep problem and more than one reason for any given sleep problem.

The problem of waking early and lacking motivation to get out of bed is most clearly associated with major depression. If you have this problem, you should see a mental health professional.

If you're having problems falling asleep, depression can again be the culprit, although it's less likely to be a debilitating major depression. Trauma survivors suffering from hyperarousal are most likely to overexert themselves or overuse alcohol in order to get themselves to sleep. Many of these people stay up late every night and still go to work in the morning—but remain chronically exhausted.

If difficulty falling asleep is your problem, relaxation training can probably help you. You can learn to relax with the help of a mental health professional through psychotherapy or biofeedback. (We'll discuss biofeedback later in this chapter.) A course in yoga or meditation will teach you to relax, or you can teach yourself through audiotapes, books, or friends. Progressive relaxation exercises with visual imagery have been shown to be very helpful in falling asleep. People with difficulty falling asleep should avoid caffeine, vigorous physical activity too close to bedtime, and daytime naps. Get into bed only when sleepy, use the bedroom only for sleep and sex, and get up at the same time every morning.

Awakening in the middle of the night is a different problem. It can also be caused by depression and could require medication, but it's very important to know *why* you're waking up, since there are different medical approaches for different problems. Some trauma survivors have anxiety attacks in their sleep. What do you feel when you awaken at night? Are you anxious, or simply unable to sleep? Do you have traumatic dreams? If so, your primary trauma needs to be talked about.

Some people awaken as a result of their state of hyperarousal, because they're startled by something. Relaxation training tends to help such people more than medication. Even if your awakening is due to depression or anxiety, it may not be severe enough to warrant medication. You and your physician must make that decision. In any case, if you're awake for more than fifteen or twenty minutes, get out of bed. The bed should be reserved for sleeping and not become associated with lying awake.

Physical Help for Physical Problems

Physical problems demand a concrete approach, something more than just talking, whether in psychotherapy or therapeutic talking with loved ones. People with very pronounced physical problems need physical relief, and until that relief arrives, talking and processing the trauma do not seem terribly relevant. Let's look at the forms of physical relief that are available from professionals and from various organizations.

Medications

Here is my philosophy on the use of medications for relief from depression and anxiety:

1.   Go to a *psychiatrist* to be evaluated for medication.   Many internists and family practitioners will prescribe minor tranquilizers and antidepressants for psychological conditions. But psychiatrists are trained to know more about psychological conditions and are more familiar with the drugs used to treat them. If you get your medications from your family doctor, there's less of a chance that psychotherapy will accompany the medications.

2.   You should be in psychotherapy if you're taking medications.   That means you should be regularly seeing and talking to a professional—either the psychiatrist supplying the medication or another therapist.

3.   You and your physician should make the decision together.   If the physician just throws the pills at you and says to take them, you may want to look for another physician. A good psychiatrist will explain the pros and cons of using medication and will

follow your use of medications carefully to deal with
any unwanted side effects.

Unfortunately, most mood-altering drugs—such as antidepressants and tranquilizers—have undesirable side effects, which vary in their impact from individual to
individual. It can take time to find the best medication for
you, and during that time, your physician should stay abreast
of the situation. Whether or not you're in personal therapy
with your physician, you need to feel you trust her and that
she is accessible.

As I indicated in the discussion on sleep problems, my
approach to using medications is conservative. There's not
really an exact point at which medications should automati-
cally be used. It varies with the individual; some people wish
to hold off on using medications, when others want the help
right away. Obviously, there does come a point where medications absolutely must be used, but it's not far from the
point where hospitalization is required.

If you have a problem with alcohol or drug abuse, be
particularly conservative in your approach to mood-altering
drugs. Many of them can interact with alcohol, magnifying
its effects and possibly producing life-threatening consequences.

You'll find that psychiatrists vary considerably in how
much they use medications. Some try to solve every problem
through drugs and view all problems as biological problems.
They're really no different from the people who think symptoms of traumatization only occur among people whose personalities predispose them. But other psychiatrists will
evaluate whether there's a biological component (such as a
family history of depression) to your symptoms. They will not
approach your case with preconceived ideas about this, and
they may or may not prescribe medications for you.

I encourage you to pursue nondrug solutions—such as
relaxation training or exercise—to manage anxiety. If your
anxiety is so extreme that you can't function adequately, you
may need tranquilizers. But that's not often the case.

On the other hand, antidepressants do have an important place in the treatment of stress disorders. If you're severely depressed, literally slowed down to a crawl, it can be very difficult to get out of your rut long enough to do things that make you feel better. If you have significant physical symptoms of depression (such as mental or physical lethargy, difficulty keeping your mind on the topic, sleep problems, and appetite and weight changes), you should at least discuss the possibility of medication with a qualified professional. And if you have emotional symptoms of depression, you should be talking with a qualified professional about that, whether or not you're interested in medication.

Antidepressants come in different classes with different levels of impact and are suited for different kinds of depression. The effects of some antidepressants may be similar to those of tranquilizers, but they're not the same. Tranquilizers treat anxiety, while antidepressants treat depression. Antidepressants with a short-acting sedating effect have been found to be very helpful with many of the hyperarousal-induced sleep problems of people with PTSD. If taken at bedtime, the medication wears off in time for the person to function the next day. A person with severe PTSD, with arousal-related insomnia and symptoms of depression, might profit from being on more than one kind of antidepressant at a time. But decisions like these should only be made in consultation with a *psychiatrist*.

Some types of antidepressant (MAO inhibitors) require a very strict diet and should not be used if you are too impulsive or are poorly disciplined. Be honest with yourself and your physician if you aren't likely to be able to follow strict dietary—including drinking—restrictions.

Behavioral Techniques

The purpose of behavior therapy is to change behavior that has been *learned*, using the techniques that help patients learn new ways of coping with their symptoms. These techniques are most effective when directed at very specific, identifiable problems, particularly those that involve anxiety. A number have proved useful in treating symptoms of PTSD, such as relaxation training, guided imagery, systematic desensitization, flooding, role playing, and biofeedback.

Relaxation Training

Relaxation training teaches you to let go of your constant need to remain in control. It utilizes muscular relaxation exercises but produces a feeling of freedom from trying to stay in control. It's like learning to float in water—you must relax, not struggle, to allow your natural buoyancy to work. Giving up that sense of control isn't easy if you're used to staying on guard every minute, anticipating a recurrence of the trauma around every corner. As you begin to relax, you may experience a panicky feeling of losing control, similar to the feeling of helplessness that goes with your trauma. But in relaxation training, you learn to give up muscular control and see that you need not feel helpless just because you completely relax your guard.

Once you have learned relaxation techniques, you can practice them on your own, sometimes with the aid of audio-tapes. Within a short period of time, you can learn to relax more quickly, even at stolen moments during the day, simply by sitting in a chair and adopting a restful posture for a few moments. You may want to use little cues to remind yourself, such as placing a colored dot on your desk to remind you to relax your shoulders or hold your fingers in a way that you have learned to associate with a state of relaxation. Relaxation training is a basic skill necessary for employing other behavioral techniques. Any behaviorally trained therapist will be able to provide you with relaxation training.

Guided Imagery

In guided imagery, a kind of relaxation technique, a therapist describes images for you to imagine. Rather than focusing on the tension in your muscles, you focus on your mind. You will be led through a series of images that are designed to relax you and restore in you a feeling of security. As with the muscular relaxation techniques, you learn cues that allow you to create restful images quickly. The difference between muscular relaxation and guided imagery techniques is like the difference between the physical relaxation of yoga postures and the mental rejuvenation of meditation. Both imagery and meditation work better when they are combined with muscular relaxation. Many therapists who utilize guided imagery, by the way, also do hypnosis.

Systematic Desensitization

Systematic desensitization is one of the best-established techniques for treating unrealistic fears. It places you in a state of relaxation and *gradually* exposes you to reminders of what you fear. Gradually you become able to deal with even the more powerful reminders without getting anxious. This process has been very helpful for people with phobias, who are excessively fearful about one particular thing. It can also be helpful in dealing with traumatic memories. As you become desensitized to the memories, running into reminders of the trauma no longer stimulates a lot of anxiety.

A similar desensitization occurs during the *processing* of traumatic events. As you process the trauma and get more comfortable talking about it, it loses some of its power to provoke anxiety in you.

If you want to try systematic desensitization, you must seek out a trained behavior therapist. It is not a skill that all therapists possess.

Flooding

Like systematic desensitization, flooding involves exposing you to reminders of your fear while you're in a state of relaxation. But where systematic desensitization tries to *slowly* accustom you to the traumatic memory without causing much anxiety and backs off when you feel anxious, flooding techniques allow the stimulus to create as much anxiety as possible. You are repeatedly exposed to it until it loses its power to provoke your anxiety. A woman who was raped in an elevator, for example, might be directed to imagine being in an elevator alone with a man who is staring at her. She would be directed to imagine similar scenes until they fail to evoke anxiety in her.

Role Playing

Role playing is used to help patients prepare for interpersonal situations that produce anxiety. Trauma survivors who have difficulty dealing with authority figures, for example, might practice situations in which they have to deal with authority figures. Role playing is useful in learning to be assertive, in controlling anger and anxiety, and in handling interpersonal conflict. A wide variety of therapists use role playing; it's particularly common in group therapy.

Biofeedback

Biofeedback is a technique in which you learn to relax by monitoring your physiological state, giving you a better ability to identify when you're relaxing and when you're speeding up. The goal is to increase your awareness of your states of tension and relaxation and your control over those states. If you take your pulse, breathe and relax, and find that it slows down your heart rate, you have used a basic biofeedback technique.

Small versions of biofeedback devices are available, and some therapists utilize these devices in their offices. But most serious biofeedback work is done in laboratories with larger machinery. When you go to a biofeedback lab, you are placed in a comfortable chair and trained to relax while you watch a monitor that tells you how you're doing. The monitoring devices vary, and some wires may be put on your head or your hand, to measure such things as muscular tension, skin temperature, or your skin's conductivity to electricity (which is affected by your perspiration).

It can be very encouraging to discover how much control you can have over events that are usually unconscious. Biofeedback has been shown to be particularly effective in dealing with headaches. You're most likely to find adequate biofeedback treatment in a large clinic, particularly a clinic associated with a hospital or educational setting.

Examples of Coping with Physical Symptoms

In this chapter, we've discussed daily stress, unhealthy mechanisms for coping with stress, and the importance of changing your niche and doing tangible, physical things for your physical problems. I haven't offered examples of actual patients in this chapter because many of these coping strategies (except for the behavior therapy techniques) don't have a one-to-one relationship with specific problems. Rather, I recommended a number of sweeping changes that you can make in your life-style that can help you deal with the physical manifestations of stress. But the following are some examples of things that people have done to overcome their physical symptoms of traumatization.

Mickey, a well-to-do young man, had led a relatively easy life. He was very large and had played football in high school. After college, he went into the family business and rose rapidly to a position of prominence. Then one night he was robbed at gunpoint and felt his life was in danger. It was the first time he'd ever been in a situation where he had absolutely no control whatsoever. Afterward, he developed a number of physical symptoms, including startle response, sleep problems, and anxiety attacks. He frequently awoke in the middle of the night in a panic and was unable to go back to sleep. As a result, he took to eating and drinking heavily and gained more than sixty pounds in one year.

Mickey tried to control his problem drinking but was unable to stop it. Finally, he sought the help of a therapist, and together they devised a plan of the changes that Mickey needed to make in his daily life. The therapist also taught

Mickey deep muscle relaxation and breathing exercises. They used a combination of relaxation and imagery techniques so that he could systematically reexperience the terror of the robbery. Eventually, Mickey reached the point where he could discuss the experience without starting to sweat and insisting on stopping. They also worked on developing cues for Mickey to use when he did relaxation on his own. He listened to audiotapes of the therapist's voice and sat in certain postures that he had come to associate with a state of relaxation.

Mickey started on a program of diet and exercise and stopped drinking. He attended Alcoholics Anonymous meetings and went to some Overeaters Anonymous lectures. Eventually, he started running and began to lose weight and get into shape. He felt much more as he had when he played football. Finally in shape, his confidence restored, he found that he no longer even wanted to drink. When he encountered something that stirred up his anxiety, he went running or did breathing and relaxation techniques. His startle response faded, and he was able to sleep again, even though reminders of the robbery continued to evoke considerable anxiety in him.

Randy, the policeman who was traumatized on his high-stress job, developed a number of physical symptoms, including anxiety attacks, when he encountered reminders of his work. He reacted very poorly to daily stress, becoming irritable and overreacting to little problems with his wife. He didn't sleep well and was continually on the verge of exhaustion. Before the job finally became too much for him, he had pursued physical exercise to the point that he was damaging his body. He was running so many miles each week that he lost considerable weight and wasn't eating the food necessary to support this demanding regimen. When he hurt his knees running, he felt so depressed that he resumed it quickly, which made his knees worse. He was eventually forced to give up running, which was a major loss, and ultimately he felt he just couldn't keep at his job.

The first hurdle for Randy was to accept that his high-stress job was too much for him. This was very difficult for him to do since he came from a family of policemen. He saw his traumatization as an indication that he was a wimp who just couldn't hack it. He gave no credit to the fact that he had spent six years on a highly intense, inner-city tactical unit and had seen more violence and dealt with more stressful situations in that short time than any of his policeman relatives had encountered in their entire careers. Indeed, a huge number of his peers from that unit became drug dependent, divorced, and stressed out, and two committed suicide. But despite all this, Randy still expected that he should be able to experience such stress without being affected by it. Eventually, he realized that he had to leave.

Once Randy accepted the need to make this most important niche change, he was more quickly able to pursue a number of lesser changes. He looked for something to replace his career and ended up going back to school to study architecture, a subject he had enjoyed but abandoned fourteen years before to enter the police force. While going to school, he busied himself in his home workshop and began to produce woodwork that he was able to sell to local businesses. He put his woodworking skills together with his wife's artistic skills, and together they produced fancy lamps and other artistic forms that sold successfully. Randy found this hobby to be enormously relaxing but made a choice to keep it as a hobby rather than turn it into a new career. He continued his studies in architecture and got a job in the field shortly after completing them.

Randy missed his old athletic pursuits, but he felt that it would be a mistake to try to resume his former frantic pace. He did not go back to running. Instead, he explored new territory and ended up taking classes in tai chi, a martial art whose goal is the development of inner calm more than outward aggression. Randy found it to be a soothing and "centering" experience, and he also took classes in meditation.

Randy also found that his friendships changed, especially those with policemen. This was particularly difficult for him. He didn't abandon these friendships but he wasn't as interested in pursuing them as he had been before. He had feared that he had nothing in common with anyone and would not make new friends, but to his surprise he discovered that he already knew many other kinds of people and that they were interested in knowing him better. Randy is a good example of someone who changed his niche, eliminated a lot of the stress in his life, and developed new ways of dealing with stress.

Lynn's traumatization occurred outside of her stressful job. After she was mugged, she developed anxiety symptoms when she had to leave home, particularly on plane trips to other cities, which her job required. She had considerable responsibility in her job, and insufficient personnel to accomplish all the work. Instead of confronting her superiors about the way her position was set up, she worked nights and weekends to get everything done herself and ended up in a constant state of exhaustion. But she had trouble getting to sleep. She dealt with both this and her anxiety by drinking wine in the evenings. Due to her exhausted physical condition and lowered resistance, she caught every virus that came along. Her mugging was a frightening memory, but it was her daily stress that was wearing her down.

Lynn, too, had been quite athletic before her traumatization. Now her physical condition deteriorated. Like Randy, it took her time before she was able to turn things around. She did it not through one major move but a series of minor ones. She moved to a part of town where the crime rate was lower and where a friend lived. She replaced the wine with an exercise class and took up tennis at a local health club. She made a number of trips to her grandparents' old farm; this was not only a powerful emotional experience but a chance to get out into the fresh air and hike in the countryside. On a physical level, Lynn began to recover her athletic condition and resistance to disease.

Lynn also made changes in her job situation. As she began to feel stronger, she asserted herself at work and insisted on better support for herself and her staff. As her work situation improved, she freed up some time to pursue a social life. She arranged to have a weekly massage and, in other ways, took better care of herself. She joined the choir at church and made new friends. Her anxieties returned occasionally, but she learned to deal with them by talking to friends and engaging in various activities. As a result, the episodes of anxiety didn't last as long. Her health was noticeably better, her sleep problems disappeared, and she felt she now knew how to deal with stress on a daily basis.

These examples show you the range of things you can do to change your niche and find better ways of dealing with stress. As usual, the people in the examples had relatively extreme traumas, but the underlying issues are similar for *all* kinds of traumatization. If you've been through a traumatic divorce or a financial upheaval, you may find that daily stress is exacting a greater toll on you than you should be paying. The kinds of changes I've described in this chapter will help you cope better with your physical reaction to stress. In the next chapter, we'll examine ways of improving your *emotional* reaction to stress.

9

REPAIRING THE DAMAGE
TO THE SENSE OF SELF
Feeling Whole Again

In Chapter 2, we saw that traumatized people inevitably sustain damage to their basic sense of self. This damage is reflected in their inability to function effectively at work and in relationships, and in their difficulty maintaining a sense of harmony and emotional balance. All these areas influence—and are in turn influenced by—self-esteem.

When you have good self-esteem, you not only think well of yourself, you have confidence in your entire environment, including how you fit into it. But when your sense of self has been damaged by traumatization, you lose the feeling of fitting in and belonging. You become at odds with your environment and question your place in it. The damage to your sense of self is aggravated by being around people who don't acknowledge the emotional shock with which you're struggling.

You need someone with whom you can talk and process

the trauma, since many traumas are just too much to reexperience and examine alone. Recovery requires both finding the appropriate relationships and being able to use them. And using relationships in this therapeutic fashion requires trust in yourself as well as the other person. We don't know exactly how processing emotional trauma in a trust relationship rebuilds a damaged sense of self, but we can see the results. You may have no close relationships, or you may be unable to take advantage of those you do have. But there are things you can do to improve your ability to enter into a close relationship.

In order for trust to develop, you must have confidence both in yourself and in the other person. The only way your confidence in yourself can grow is for you to build your self-esteem and learn to control your anger and defensiveness. Then you must take the risk of letting someone matter enough to have an influence on you.

Self-esteem is not a static thing—it's a dynamic process that lives and breathes, ebbs and flows according to how a person's life is going. Whether you realize it or not, you have a great capacity to influence your own self-esteem; you can either strengthen or damage it. If you listen to your inner voice, you may find that you say things to yourself that interfere with your self-esteem. You may put yourself down and call yourself names—"Boy, am I stupid"—or you may maintain unrealistic expectations and standards for yourself, such as "I should always be on top of every situation."

How can you change these patterns? Learn to replace your negative self-talk with positive self-talk—"I handled that pretty well"—and make your standards and goals *realistic*, based on accurate views of yourself. Recognize your limitations, and work with them instead of fighting them. Don't chide yourself for having limitations; rather, congratulate yourself for knowing how to live with them. Most of all, listen to what you're saying to yourself. Are you being hard on yourself? If so, that's where you want to substitute more encouraging comments.

Altering Your Life

Changing your self-talk can go a long way toward improving your self-esteem. But in itself it's not enough. You must also change how you behave. The source of your self-esteem is yourself, so you're the one who can make you feel good about yourself. And you're the judge of what you really need to do in order to accomplish this.

So the thing you need to do is to identify and change the things that make you feel bad about yourself. Once you have identified something that you don't like about yourself, examine the conditions where you tend to do it. At what critical point in the events leading up to it do you normally *decide* to do it? If you feel bad about your tendency to procrastinate, for example, and put off doing the difficult things and do the easy things first, that critical decision point occurs when you are deciding what to do with your time. In order to change, you have to decide to do the difficult things first. Then the whole process is altered. Once you isolate that critical decision point, you can change the bad habit and improve your self-esteem.

Working on a *goal* is the best way to put your self-discipline into gear. If you're a workaholic, your goal may be to spend more time pursuing leisure activities. If you're not working enough, your goal may be to take on new projects. If you feel your life is stagnating, your goal may be to develop new interests. If your life is overwhelming, your goal may be to prioritize your time and set limits. But wherever you start, the purpose of setting a goal is to make your life better. It gives you a sense of direction—something concrete to work on, and something concrete to point to and feel good about.

Here are some suggestions for how you can go about altering your life in a positive fashion:

- Step back and take an overview. Is there something you are *not* doing that you probably should be doing? Or are you doing something that you probably should not be doing?

- What are your bad habits? Are any of those habits truly interfering with your being what you would like to be?

- Where would you prefer to be at this point in your life? Is there a central project (such as starting an exercise program, going to school, or stopping drinking) that would lead in that direction?

- Think about setting some goals. Make a list of all the goals you'd like to accomplish. Consider which of those goals would allow you to overcome your disappointment in yourself. Number those goals according to their priority.

- Don't overwhelm yourself by trying to achieve all your goals at once. Focus on one, maybe two. Pick one that's important—it doesn't have to be the highest on your list. Rather, it should be one that you feel you have a chance of accomplishing.

- Now break your goal down into steps. Write down every aspect of achieving that goal. Make a realistic plan for achieving the goal, including isolating and changing that central decision-making point.

- Show your plan to your loved ones. Get their support for achieving your goal. And talk to them as you pursue your goal; keep them informed.

- When you've accomplished your goal, give yourself a reward. Don't let it go unnoticed—take some time to feel good about what you've done.

- Then go back to your list and decide what's next.

Some problems with self-esteem are deep-seated; solving them requires more than these simple steps can provide. But even with deep-seated problems, these steps bring some improvement. And the better your self-esteem becomes, the more you'll be able to pursue the other aspect of repairing your damaged sense of self—engaging in trust relationships.

Defensiveness versus Vulnerability

In every important relationship in your life, you have a choice—you can be vulnerable, or you can be defensive. If you're vulnerable, you let the other person (and yourself) know what your feelings are—particularly weak, frightened feelings. But if you're defensive, you hide those vulnerable feelings. You blame the other person whenever there's a conflict. You get angry instead of hurt. Your focus is on how the other person is behaving, what he or she is doing to you and making you feel. You don't acknowledge your own part in the conflicts or in maintaining the distance between you.

If you're defensive, your relationship is perpetually less than satisfying. You always feel that there should be more, that there's something wrong. It doesn't restore you—it drains you. If you're vulnerable, however, you can get hurt, perhaps very badly. If you've been hurt much in the past, you're likely to shy away from being vulnerable now. If you were traumatized and others responded poorly, a second traumatization occurred—to your relationships and to your social sense of yourself. But you can redevelop your trust in others only by being vulnerable, by taking the risk of getting hurt. If you start out from a defensive position, you don't really know what the other person is capable of because you haven't given him a chance.

Helen and Rich had been happily married for seventeen years when Rich discovered that Helen had been having affairs off and on for the past twelve years. He was devastated by his discovery, and his world disintegrated. Everything he thought he knew and trusted was thrown into doubt. Helen, for her part, seemed relieved to finally be able to tell him the truth. Over the years, she had built a wall of lies between them, starting with small lies and snowballing into a mountain of lies. Indeed, her philandering was probably increased by the lies, because the more lies she placed between herself and her husband, the more distant she felt from him. Now she was relieved to no longer have to work at juggling the many falsehoods.

Once the truth came out, her affairs stopped. Helen and Rich entered marital therapy and worked on rebuilding their trust relationship. But the biggest hurdle for Rich was to risk trusting his wife once more. That would have meant exposing himself to the possibility of getting badly hurt again. So he remained defensive to protect himself. He constantly criticized and argued with Helen, finding something wrong in everything she said and did.

Both of them thought that he was critical and argumentative because he was still angry over the philandering. But I don't think that was the primary reason. Rich was protecting himself from getting hurt again. He remained defensive by constantly being on the offense and focusing on Helen rather than his own vulnerable feelings.

If you want to overcome your defensiveness, it helps to be able to recognize the ways you maintain it. Here are some common ways people avoid becoming vulnerable in a relationship:

- *Fault finding.* Since everyone is human, you'll seldom be disappointed in your search for the other person's faults. You'll feel justified in maintaining your attitude that no one is the right person to trust.

- *Constant conflict.* As long as you're fighting, it's impossible to stop being defensive. So if you're afraid to reveal your vulnerable feelings, you can start a fight. That will keep you from having to reveal a vulnerable feeling.

- *Grievance collecting.* In order to keep conflict alive and avoid resolving anything, you can collect grievances. One sin always reminds you of other sins, so you can maintain ready access to the anger you need to hang in there and stay defensive. No transgression is ever forgiven.

- *Withdrawal.* If you don't feel up to constant conflict, you can just withdraw—physically or emotionally—in order to keep a distance from the other person and thereby protect your more vulnerable feelings.

- *Investing in things.* If it's difficult to withdraw emotionally and be unfeeling around others, you can disguise your withdrawal by investing yourself in things instead of people. You can expend your energy working or playing to a degree that cuts others out of your life.

- *Being superficial.* If you must spend time with others but you're afraid to be vulnerable and you don't want conflict, you can always just be terribly superficial. Talk about anything *except* how you feel and what's going on between the two of you. Sports and the weather are acceptable as elevator conversation, but they tend to run a little dry when that's all you have to say to someone important to you.

- *Avoiding the here and now.* The most vulnerable feelings are the ones you're actually feeling as you talk about them. It's easier to talk about feelings in the past tense or as if they occurred in some other time and place.

And here are some things you can do to make the shift from being defensive to being more vulnerable:

- Make *I* statements. When you and your loved one are talking about the hot topics, don't start each sentence with *you*. Talk about yourself rather than focusing on her.

- Express your feelings. Focus inside yourself and determine what you're feeling. Then listen to what you say. Are you really expressing feelings (like sadness, loneliness, longing, and fear), or are you expressing thoughts preceded by the words *I feel*?

- Don't give in to your angry feelings. You're angry because of something—find that thing and express it. Has your loved one said or done something that left you feeling unloved, hurt, sad, or cut off from her?

- When you express that feeling, don't blame your loved one because you feel that way. Chances are that your loved one touched on a vulnerable feeling that was already there and simply brought it to life. Help her know where your vulnerabilities are so that she can tread more carefully.

- Stay in the "here and now." Don't let your discussion range into all the past ways you've been hurt by each other. That will likely be too much and bring back your defensiveness.

- If you feel overwhelmed and need to withdraw, state your need directly. Own it as *your* need, not as something you have to do because she's so difficult.

Rage

Rage is another barrier to getting close to others. I don't list it as one of the ways we stay defensive and avoid vulnerability because I don't think it is that kind of mechanism. Anger certainly feeds defensiveness, but rage is more than anger—it is anger out of control. It may frighten the angry person as much as it frightens his target. It feels as if it has a life of its own. Rage generally accompanies a damaged sense of self and is a frequent symptom of traumatization, particularly when there's a secondary trauma. While not all trauma survivors have attacks of rage, most either do or feel the rage inside and fear losing control of it. In general, men give vent to their rage more than women.

There are at least two types of rage that trauma survivors experience. One results from the feeling of helplessness produced by the primary trauma. That feeling of helplessness is intolerable, and you'll do anything to change it. When you're enraged, you don't feel helpless. Instead, you suddenly feel powerful and in control.

The second type of rage is an aspect of the secondary trauma. It expresses a trauma survivor's reaction to the breakdown in his relationship with his social world. In some invisible way, we're all connected to a personal community of people, and when this connection is healthy, we weather life's disruptions. It is *communities* of people who survive, form cultures, and thrive. The secondary trauma occurs if you lose your sense of being connected to the people around you. It can feel as if the group has released their hold of you and left you on your own. Your rage is at the group for not caring enough to hold on to you when you need it.

Normally people can feel connected even through conventional casual contacts like elevator talk. You can also feel connected through mediums such as reading, watching television, or listening to music. But if you have been traumatized and suffered a breakdown in your social world, you've lost that ability to feel easily connected. Now you need a special trusting connection to help you repair your damaged sense of self. You need a more intense, responsive contact than elevator talk.

Controlling Rage Attacks

In order to reestablish your sense of being connected, you must control your rage and enter into a trust relationship. To understand your rage better it helps to compare it with the tantrums of children. Those tantrums don't just appear out of nowhere—they're usually a response to something, such as stress, tiredness, or unconnectedness. After a period of dissatisfaction and little episodes of control battles with the adult, the child blows up. Afterward, the child can't be approached for a while; she's sad and wants to be left alone. Eventually, she's ready to resume normal activities. Adults understand that her tantrum is over when she makes an effort to reconnect.

Adults go through something similar when they experience a rage attack. The episode usually begins with a period of dissatisfaction or irritation; sometimes you may be feeling very good, only to have some disappointment or frustration plunge you backward. When you blow up, you temporarily sever your feeling of connectedness to your loved one. As a result, her arguments have no effect upon you, which is very perplexing for her because she can't understand how your caring for her could suddenly just cease. After the rage attack, you feel sad and find it difficult to reconnect. But the feeling that you do want to reconnect is a sign that your rage is gone.

If you live with someone and find yourself getting enraged with her, despite your wish to control your temper, it can help if both of you understand what's setting you off. It also helps to know the stages of your rage. After a fight, if your loved one tries to reconnect before your rage has run its course, it can easily reactivate the fight.

Reconnecting is very difficult for some couples. They cool down from a conflict—and become ready to reconnect —at different rates. The one who's ready to reconnect first often restimulates the fight by trying to reconnect too soon and not respecting the fact that the other isn't ready yet. Then the first one gets angry all over again, and the cycle continues.

Mark and Annette were traumatized when Mark developed cancer. The illness virtually exhausted their financial resources, but they managed to recover. Now Mark's illness is in remission, but they live with the constant stress of knowing it can return. The bout with cancer had a great impact on their relationship. They got much closer for a while, then began having frequent arguments. Mark would become enraged and often threaten to leave. Annette was terribly hurt by the threats and the other things he would say when he lost his temper.

Both of them would get angry during the fights, but Annette would always cool down more quickly and approach Mark to be friends again. But this would lead to another flareup. Mark would make some reference to the point of contention, and Annette would try to restate what she'd said in a more acceptable and understandable way. He would interpret this as a refusal to let it go, which made him even more defensive, and on it would go.

Their fights often centered on Mark's concerns about his health. Annette felt he needed to stop talking so much about it, and she communicated this indirectly by changing the subject, by disagreeing with him about minor aspects of what he was saying, or by minimizing what he was saying. ("Oh, Mark, thousands of people have had that symptom and nothing was wrong.") This made Mark feel she didn't care. But when she learned to say *directly* that she didn't want to talk about it, things improved—though not before they went through an initial period of increased tension. And when Mark learned to express his feeling that she didn't care instead of threatening to leave, that helped even more. Most important, Mark got a handle on his blowups.

Mark worked on his tendency to blow up in couples therapy with Annette. He learned that he was approaching her with expectations of understanding and support. When he felt he didn't get that understanding and support, he would feel crushed with helplessness and disappointment. Then he'd swing quickly from expecting understanding from her to expecting the worst from her.

Once his trust collapsed, he would protect his vulnerable feelings of disappointment by going on the offensive and getting angry and making threats. In therapy, however, he learned to hold back on the threats and not do the kinds of things that would escalate the argument. Most important, he learned to express his disappointment and feelings of helplessness *instead* of blowing up. And Annette was able to respond to these feelings with the understanding he wanted.

If you have rage attacks, here are some things you can do:

1. Start by reminding yourself that you really do want to maintain your connection, even though you

may lose track of it in the middle of conflicts. Make a rule that you'll overcome your reluctance to reconnect and try to keep your connection with your loved one, even when you're angry.

2.   Learn to recognize when you're in that preliminary state of feeling dissatisfied, short-tempered, or grumpy. Once you recognize it, let your loved one know that you're in a bad mood and need to be left alone.

3.   Learn to calm yourself during the key period when the situation usually escalates into a blowup. Use breathing exercises, meditation, exercise, or whatever soothing activities you've found.

4.   Slow down. Look for the sadness, the helplessness, the loneliness—the vulnerable feelings—and learn to express those.

5.   If you do blow up, try to bring more control to the things you do and say while you're enraged. Part of you knows that you will regret these things later. Listen to that part of yourself.

6.   If you're enraged, say what you're angry about, then leave it alone.

7.   You may need to get away from your loved one for a period of time in order to calm yourself down. If so, let her know that you are not abandoning her but just need some solitude to calm down.

8.   Learn to recognize your own oblique feelings of wanting to reconnect. It's fear that prevents you from acting on those feelings. Learn to reach out.

Improvement begins with a decrease in the *frequency* of rage episodes, not with a decrease in their intensity. They may occur less often, but they can be just as intense as ever. So don't let the intensity of an occasional rage attack make you think you're not making progress. They can be stopped, but it takes time. Be patient and work at controlling your rage.

The Overall Picture of Recovery

Successful recovery is reflected in the reestablishment of your sense of connection and belonging to the social world around you. As I indicated in Chapter 4, a traumatized person tends to withdraw from society in levels and return in reverse order, usually starting with intimate relations and moving outward.

Recovery from both the primary and secondary traumas involves utilizing a trust relationship with another person or persons. It's easier to reexperience and examine the primary trauma when you feel connected to someone who cares and understands. Only in an intimate relationship can your sense of self and of connection be fully restored.

You can do things to make it easier for you to engage in a trust relationship. You can work directly on your self-esteem, which, ironically, contributes to your ability to trust others. You can make efforts to overcome your particular ways of remaining defensive and avoiding vulnerability. And you can work to understand and control your feelings of rage, which may be expressed *or* hidden under the surface.

Several other things can aid the process of recovery while you work things out in your trust relationships. If you have physical symptoms that are getting in the way, deal with them directly rather than just waiting for them to disappear as a result of processing the trauma.

And there are other things you can do to facilitate your healing process. The next chapter is about a different way of approaching the processing and letting go of the trauma. It's about taking advantage of the power of healing rituals.

10

HEALING RITUALS

It was a quiet spring day in Washington, D.C. The parks were busy but not yet crowded with the throngs of summer tourists. At the Vietnam Veterans Memorial, the people in front of the Wall moved very slowly, if at all. When they spoke, it was in hushed, almost reverent tones, like tourists at a religious monument. The top of the Wall is at ground level; the panels are highest in the center and taper down as they approach each end. This causes the observer to walk down below ground level and then back up again at the other end.

The Wall is made of a deep, black polished granite that reflects the figures standing and kneeling in front of it. The reflections become background to the names engraved in the granite. There are things on the ground leaning against the Wall—flowers here, small American flags there, letters, a figurine, an old camouflage shirt, a framed citation, and photographs. People reach out and touch the Wall, gingerly tracing a name with their fingertips. At one point, a man holds up a small boy so that he may touch a name; at another point, a teenager steadies a piece of paper while another teen rubs the side of a pencil against it to obtain a copy of the name underneath.

To the right of center, a couple with two preteen children are studying the names. The father draws his finger down a section, row by row. After a few moments, he turns and nods to his daughter, and she places a wicker basket in front of the Wall. Her mother then nods to the boy, who bends down and drops a letter and several photos into the basket. The father steps back to watch, and the mother takes his hand. The little boy stands and surveys his work, then glances up at his parents. The father releases the mother's hand and renders a brief salute. They all stand quietly a moment longer, then they turn to their right and walk slowly down the walkway.

Rituals as Structures for Healing

If you've never been to the Vietnam Veterans Memorial, the above scene may sound a little unreal. It's not. The memorial is a very spiritual place, and a lot of healing takes place there. I am particularly familiar with it, but there are many such places of healing. Societies build memorials in an effort to heal from social traumas—whether for thousands lost in a war or for one who meant so much to many, such as the memorial to John Kennedy at the point where he was shot in front of the Texas School Book Depository. We often memorialize the location of a trauma; if we don't know the actual location, then we "memorialize" one designated to represent the trauma.

We imbue the memorial with the significance of the trauma, and it takes on the power to evoke many of our feelings about the trauma. In effect, the location of the memorial —a grave, a religious structure, a monument—becomes sacred to us. In our minds, it takes on a very specific meaning, dedicated to one purpose. When others disregard the special meaning we've assigned a location, we can be terribly offended—as witnessed by the commotion over current uses of former concentration camps. That issue was raised by the people who were traumatized there and who therefore hold those locations sacred.

It helps the grieving process if we have a specific place to focus our grief and an opportunity to share it with others. We build churches and temples in order to pray together, and many people designate corners of their homes for spiritual purposes. These tangible places help us to enter domains of feeling that aren't easy to experience. We're able to experience them when we have the stimulus of going together to a funeral or laying a headstone. Much of the communication at such times is nonverbal—a hug, a pat, a squeeze, a handshake, or a caring look. Rituals prescribe some of the verbal communication, so we have a lot of help in expressing difficult feelings.

When Richard died in an auto accident, he left a wife and three children. His wife, Gloria, was very busy the day of the funeral, arranging for the family to entertain a large number of visitors afterward. A number of friends helped out by bringing food and picking up out-of-town relatives who flew in for the service. Her three children also busily helped with the preparations. At the service, Gloria was escorted to her seat by her son Philip, who was ten. The elder daughter, Melissa, who was twelve, had written a poem, which was printed up and handed out at the door. And the younger daughter, Mandy, seven, carried a rose up and laid it on her father's coffin before the service began.

When people "paid their respects" and visited after the service, considerable food and refreshments awaited them. Each guest waited his or her turn to speak to Gloria and "offer their condolences." Almost all these people shook her hand, but more often they held her hand in both of theirs and/or hugged her. It was usually during the hugs that Gloria would tear up and cry for a moment. Most of these people also spoke to the children. Several times, a number of people gathered and talked about what a fine person Richard had been. More than once, there was laughter as the conversation focused on humorous memories of Richard. Upon leaving, a number of people commented to Gloria that they would be seeing her again soon. Several families made plans to do something with Melissa, Philip, and Mandy within the coming week.

As you can see, many ritualized behaviors accompanied this funeral. The rituals weren't limited to the service itself; indeed, most of them occurred outside the actual ceremony. But from beginning to end, from the clothes worn to the food eaten, the day was full of rituals. Without them, that large number of people would not have known what to do. There would never have been such an opportunity for so many people to explicitly express their caring to this family. Rituals provided a structure for the healing that took place between these people.

The Healing Power of Rituals

Rituals are activities that serve the same function as memorials. They facilitate the processing of difficult feelings— they allow us to experience those feelings and consider the meanings of emotional issues while reducing our anxiety over what to say and do. I consider rituals to be a major element in healing from trauma. Although healing rituals often take place at established memorials, they aren't limited to them. Just as any place can be memorialized, rituals can be adapted to fit any situation.

This chapter focuses on rituals that contribute to the process of healing from traumatization, which means primarily those dealing with *loss, transition,* and *transformation.* These rituals help us to focus on selected powerful symbols; grieve the losses; relinquish life stages and periods associated with the trauma; experience and express emotions related to the trauma; and develop new ways of viewing ourselves.

Existing rituals for dealing with loss include funerals and wakes. Those for dealing with transitions include graduations and retirement dinners. And those for dealing with the transformation of a person include fasting and baptism. But these existing rituals are not the only healing rituals available to you. You can also create your own.

Creating Healing Rituals

When you create healing rituals, don't ignore those that already exist. Rather, start by thinking about ways you can draw upon the power of existing rituals and symbols and adapt them to your own healing process. Here are some of the common aspects of effective healing rituals.

1. Healing Rituals Always Involve Symbolism

The power of symbols is that they can be used to represent intangibles. A gravestone represents the intangible thing that we call a loss. A little pin on the lapel of a jacket can represent membership in a group, such as Holocaust survivors or American citizens. Once you've imbued a particular thing with the power to symbolize an intangible, you can express feelings about that intangible through the way you treat the symbol. You can slip the ring on your spouse's finger happily, or you can angrily throw it on the floor, indicating very different feelings about your marital bond. Every effective healing ritual involves symbols.

In June 1986, I participated in a very powerful public healing ritual—the Chicago Vietnam Veterans Welcome Home Parade. The vets were all decked out in symbols of their service—jungle fatigues, hats, boots, dog tags, medals, and other military insignia. Nonveterans walking in the parade held pictures over their heads as symbols of the loved ones they lost in the war. Bystanders waved flags and threw confetti from the windows to symbolize their support. These people may not have been thinking of themselves as using symbols, but they certainly were. As a result, the parade was a powerful ritual.

If the ritual is to evoke feelings about a trauma, the trauma must be symbolized as a part of the ritual. Some people actually recreate the trauma, such as by the reenactment of Civil War battles. For others, the symbol is a more passive reminder, such as the names on the Wall. Sometimes people need to perform symbolic actions with the symbol of their trauma. Rituals of burning and/or burying photos and drawings of a trauma can be helpful in putting it behind.

When Pablo, Raul, and Manuel (whom we met in Chapter 7) were asked by their therapist to draw their impressions of what had happened to their father, the therapist took each boy's drawing and locked it in his desk. The drawings were not shown to other family members. Instead, they were eventually burned in a ritual with the boys' mother Juanita and the therapist.

2. Prepare for the Ritual

The notion of preparing for the ritual is important—in fact, it's really *part* of the ritual. We build up to a ritual through a preparatory process that contributes to its power to influence us. Holiday rituals often require several days of preparation during which we decorate, cook and clean, and create symbols for the ceremony. Going through this process gets us "in the mood" and contributes to our ability to launch into the proper feelings at the time of the ceremony. It's important that everyone play a part in this preparatory process because doing so makes it much easier to experience the sharing in an effective ritual. People who show up only for the ceremony may not become integrated into the group or get as much out of the ritual. Parents intuitively know to include children in the preparatory process for rituals. Gloria's children prepared for their day of rituals in a number of ways: by dressing appropriately, writing a poem, picking out the flowers, and practicing walking down the aisle.

3. Everyone Must Be Involved

It's essential to include everyone in preparing for a ritual and in enacting it. Rituals involve action, and everyone must feel that he or she has a part to play in it. Even ordinary actions are understood to mean something extraordinary for the purpose of the ritual. For example, eating and drinking take on a very different meaning when they're performed in the Communion ritual of a Christian church. And rituals involve feelings—we feel something as a result of participating in the ritual. The feelings associated with a trauma can run the gamut, so it's not only sadness that you will see at a trauma healing ritual. Ever notice how people cry at weddings and smile at funeral receptions? Both of those rituals allow for many different feelings to be experienced. Furthermore, bear in mind that the ritual is for everyone—not just the trauma survivor—and that everyone will have feelings about the experience.

Joey's family's response to his fears about the fire is an excellent example of getting everyone involved. The entire family came up with ideas and planned the rituals of visiting the fire station, having fire drills, and playing with toy fire engines. A therapist might do these kinds of things with a child individually. But I believe a response like this by the entire family has much more immediate impact than therapy sessions with a stranger.

4. Choose the Setting for the Ritual

Locating the ritual at a site that is a reminder of the trauma can evoke the trauma without any further symbols. This site could be the place of the trauma or other locations that have been memorialized and consequently dedicated to the trauma. The timing of the ritual can also create an evocative setting; anniversaries of a trauma are times that we are inevitably reminded of it. Getting together with other survivors of the trauma establishes a similarly evocative setting. Whenever enough survivors get together, they are likely to perform some ritual in honor of the trauma—if nothing more, a toast to lost companions.

On the tenth anniversary of her traumatic abortion, Dale returned to the site of the abortion clinic with her husband Ed. They went back through all the same rooms and saw many details that had been "invisible" to Dale the first time. Afterward, they went for a quiet meal and talked about the feelings that surfaced as a result of their visit—a visit made particularly powerful by its timing.

5. Rituals of Transformation Are Seldom Easy

Rituals of transformation serve to help people change their image of themselves. But in order for a ritual to do this, you must endow that ritual with a great deal of power, like the power you give to a relationship when you allow it to matter to you. You become invested in it and you put a lot of energy into it. If a relationship or a ritual requires no effort on your part, you may take it for granted. But if you must invest yourself in it and work at it, you place greater value on it. Some rituals of transformation are physically grueling, such as the Outward Bound movement, while others draw their power from an emotional investment, such as baptism. Often you must prepare lavishly for the ceremonial part of the ritual, such as a bar mitzvah.

I think that one of the best examples of transformation rituals is the American Indian sweat lodge ceremony. It's a ritual of purification, during which the participants enter a tent filled with steam created by putting water on rocks that have been heated in a fire. It's a grueling experience that requires a deep commitment and can involve several days of preparation. It usually includes fasting and other forms of self-denial and can produce visions and altered states of consciousness. When it's over, participants report their experiences as deeply meaningful and there's an experience of having been changed.

6. The Need for Experts

Some healing rituals can be conducted with your own family or friends. But most rituals of transformation are conducted by established guides, such as a priest or a drill sergeant. Many transformation rituals are too demanding to pursue without an established guide to help you.

Colonel Bob Rheault is the innovative developer of a ritual that is used by several VA hospitals' in-patient stress units. He takes groups of Vietnam veterans with PTSD on an Outward Bound experience, climbing mountains and negotiating "confidence" courses on ropes high in the air. After a few days on these trips, many of the veterans report profound experiences of transformation. Similarly, Vietnam veterans have participated in American Indian sweat lodge ceremonies and other rituals of purification. Many find these to be profound experiences, helping them to stop thinking of themselves as victims, thereby transforming their self-images.

The "guide" in these rituals is usually someone who has already undergone the transformation and can be believed in. Colonel Rheault was at one time commander of all Special Forces in Vietnam; Indian experts were "guides" in the sweat lodge ceremonies. The ritual may not have the same power if you don't think that the guide is knowledgeable.

The implications of this requirement must be considered as you develop your own healing rituals. If you're trying to develop a ritual of transformation, it helps to include someone who is an authority on the transformation. Of course, the "guide's" authority lies in the perception of the participants. For example, some people feel properly married if a judge performs the ceremony, while others require a clergyman.

7. Your Family's Style

If you want to develop healing rituals to deal with your family's traumatization, first consider the ways your family has dealt with losses, transitions, and transformations. (And think about your family's rules concerning the expression of emotion, which we discussed in Chapter 3.) What is your unique role in the rituals? How does the nature of the ritual change your role? Here are some questions that can help you get a picture of your family's style:

Transitions and Celebrations

- What holidays do you actually celebrate (not just take off work)? Thinking about holidays usually brings an instant image of your family's holiday rituals.

- What are the typical ways your family celebrates birthdays, achievements, and transitions?

- Do such celebrations usually involve food, drink, and physical activities?

- What are the special places where you celebrate?

- Who is usually included?

- Do people sing, make speeches, give toasts, or tell stories?

- What role does each family member play? Is there a director, an audience, someone who does the majority of crying for the family or expresses all the sentiments?

- Does your family have a cultural or ethnic tradition that determines how these events are conducted?

Loss

- How does your family handle loss?

- If relatives have died, how were the ceremonies conducted?

- Who directed the ceremonial aspects of the ritual —family members or experts?

- Is it typical for everyone to talk about their feelings, or do some individuals tend to speak on behalf of all?

- What "props" are usually involved—flowers, photos, written speeches?

Transformations

- What is your family's history of transformations? What are the pervasive stories about momentous incidents in the lives of family members, particularly from your parents' time and that of earlier generations?

- Does your family emphasize educational experiences, religious experiences, or other worldly pursuits? Do your parents attribute their life choices to their belief in God, graduation from college, military service, or what?

- Are there family stories about events that changed the lives of family members, such as the summer Grandpa worked for the railroad or the time the family's home burned? If so, can you identify the rituals that the family members employed at the time?

  Now that you have some sense of your family's rituals for dealing with common losses, transitions, and transformations, consider how these elements appear in more powerful family events —like trauma.

Past Traumas

- What are the stories about past traumas your family has experienced?

- What were those traumas, and how were they handled?

- Do your parents identify the Depression or the war or some other major event as particularly significant in determining who they are today? If so, how did they (and their own families) respond to that event?

- What rituals did the family perform to overcome these historical traumas?

- Might these past traumas still be partly unresolved?

- How much does the current trauma resemble the past trauma? Is it stirring up old wounds?

My goal is not to make you obsessively concerned with how your family works. Rather, I want to increase your awareness that you already have a family legacy of rituals, rules, and patterns for dealing with loss, transition, transformation, and perhaps even traumatization. You have some of these resources available to you now. Think about how these existing resources, particularly the rituals, can be adapted to help you and your family deal with the trauma that you're currently confronting.

A Healing Ritual for Your Trauma

Now I would like to talk about actually creating a ritual for *your family* to deal with its traumatization. Your ritual should include some elements from the rituals you've developed for dealing with transition, transformation, and loss. All of these are involved in overcoming the effects of traumatization. Designing and conducting a ritual is something that you can all do together, whether you are a traumatized individual or a family member of one. Begin by gathering the tools that we've already discussed:

- the existing repertoire of rituals your family has used over the years;

- the elements of effective rituals (listed earlier); and

- the participation of everyone who is part of the family or other group that has been affected by the traumatization.

Your goal is to design rituals that address the specific traumatization that has affected your family, and to gear those rituals to the unique culture that is your family. The ritual you design will be solely yours, reflecting the unique characteristics of your family, though it may share many elements with the rituals of others.

It may be helpful to take a pencil and paper and write down your answers to each of the following eight sets of questions. Devote a full sheet of paper to each set, even if you answer only one or two questions. Once you've gone through them all, pick and choose from each page to design an appropriate ritual. Making written lists of the necessary elements can aid in the difficult task of creating the ritual.

Remember, this task will be most effective if the entire family is involved—the process of designing a family ritual can itself be part of healing. Engaging in this process may bring to the surface some of the conflicts and different perceptions among family members and give you an opportunity to reach a better mutual understanding.

1. Specify the Trauma

What exactly has traumatized your family? It helps to be precise here. Was there a specific trauma, a series of traumas, or a stressful period? Was an individual traumatized, several individuals, or the entire family? Did it involve people from outside the family? (You may want to include certain outsiders in your healing rituals.)

Identifying the specific nature of the trauma will be simple for many people, more complicated for others. But you should be able to point your finger at an event or series of events that you feel caused the trauma. If there are multiple traumas that do not cluster easily, you may need to break them down into separate traumas.

2. Specify Who Was Affected by the Trauma and How

Everyone was affected by the traumatization in some fashion, but it can be helpful to sit down and think about exactly how each family member was affected. Do some members feel unsafe, or lack trust in strangers (or in other family members)? Do they lack hopefulness about the future and illusions of security? Do they feel guilty or enraged, or simply feel stuck in the past? What particular issues has traumatization induced in each individual family member? As you identify these issues, think about what you would like a ritual to achieve for each family member.

3. Specify How the Entire Family Was Affected

What is different about the family as a whole now? Is there a general numbing of emotions, a lack of connectedness among family members, a pervasive sadness, an upsurge in conflict, a loss of intimacy, fun, or hope? Do people no longer do things that they used to do together? Has there been an increase in activities that have a low degree of sharing—such as television watching? Are individuals going outside the family more? Does the family eat together, go to religious services, or play together as much as they used to?

Again, listing these changes can help you to think concretely about what you would like a ritual to achieve for your family. You can't expect everything to change as a result of a ritual, but this list will focus your thinking and help you to plan a ritual that is relevant to your needs.

4. Specify the Existing Public Rituals Available

What existing public rituals are associated with events like the one you're trying to heal? Have you taken advantage of these existing rituals? If your trauma was public and affected others, have you attended memorial services, visited sacred sites, or otherwise participated in organized ceremonies? If not, why not? It is very important to answer this question. Do your family members have attitudes that make it difficult for them to take advantage of the public healing rituals? Such attitudes must be identified and discussed; they can interfere in your own rituals as well as prevent you from getting something out of the public ones.

5. Develop Symbols for the Trauma

Once you have identified the trauma and its effects, think about ways to symbolize the trauma. A loss can be symbolized by finding or creating a reminder of what was lost. Often a loss is quite tangible, but the beauty of symbols is that losses that are actually intangible can be given tangible reminders. Thus, the loss of illusions of security might be symbolized by an unlocked door, a picture of a child confidently leaping into a parent's arms, or a photo of an infant sleeping peacefully. The loss of dreams might be symbolized by a facsimile of a diploma, a model of a building that was planned, a clipping about a successful athlete, or a series of pictures of a child growing up or a couple growing old together.

Most of the healing rituals you design will involve symbols of what has been lost and probably symbols of change, but they may not include the idea of transition and transformation. But if you're trying to put together one major ritual for your family, I urge you to create one that includes all three components. Your survivor will only profit from an "ordeal" if she finds it meaningful—not just an arbitrary idea that you came up with. Placing the healing ritual in the broader framework of transformation can help to "legitimize" your endeavor.

Symbols for transitions, as the completion of a life stage, usually include symbols of both the old stage and the new. It is cadets throwing their old hats into the air, to be replaced with new hats with a different insignia. A rape survivor might wear two roses, onc closed and one open to symbolize her transition from being withdrawn and fearful back to feeling more open and uninhibited. It is "something old, something new"—a traditional symbol of change.

Transformations are symbolized by the old-new symbol

of the transition and by a symbol of the ordeal of the trans-formation itself. The ordeal aspect may be largely symbolic, such as being held underwater in a baptism, or it may be quite demanding, as in the sweat lodge ceremony. But it's there to show that the individual has put himself through a grueling process in order to achieve this transformation. A transformation can not simply be awarded—it must be earned.

6. Perform Symbolic Actions of Parting with the Past

One of the primary goals of a healing ritual—after ac-knowledging the trauma and reexperiencing it—is to accept the fact of the traumatization, then let it go. For example, the flag used in a military funeral is folded and given to the next of kin—it is taken out of use and put away permanently. When you enact rituals of loss and transition, you symbolize what was lost, then you bury it, destroy it, give it away, or otherwise indicate that it's no longer part of your life. When you symbolize losing something during a ritual, you say good-bye to it. This action helps you resolve your grief and relinquish the past so that you can be more open to the fu-ture.

7. Perform Symbolic Actions of Becoming Something New

It's easier to relinquish the past if you have something to replace it with—or else you'll have little motivation to give it up. You must feel that you have a future if you're really going to overcome your traumatization. A symbol can help you rec-ognize and accept the differences between the past and the future. For example, the family that loses a member stands together at the funeral—symbolizing the new family that they have become. They're not just the old family without a mem-ber, they're a new family—a smaller one. If a person loses the use of his legs, a wheelchair may come to symbolize part of who he is now. It need not be only a reminder of what he has lost; it can represent the way he gets around now.

Many families find it easier to symbolize what was lost

than to symbolize what lies ahead. Leaving an empty place at the table for the one who is gone is a powerful symbol of the loss and can mobilize the sadness. But the family that continues to eat with that empty place at the table sits too far apart to function as a family. In order to function now, they must remove the empty place and establish a new seating arrangement. To do this effectively, they may have to remove a leaf from the table or even buy a new table.

8. Plan the Ritual as a Family

The plans for the ritual must specify every person's part in it. Some parts may be much smaller than others, but it's terribly important that everyone participate. When Mandy placed the flower on her father's casket, she participated every bit as much as the adult who delivered the eulogy.

Examples of Healing Rituals

The kinds of healing rituals people create are as varied as the traumas themselves. Some take advantage of existing formal rituals conducted by community institutions such as churches. Others create their own unique rituals with highly defined roles for everyone involved. Still others perform informal rituals that occur spontaneously in settings that tend to remind them of the trauma.

You're likely to pursue your own healing ritual in the ways to which you are most accustomed—formal or informal, unique or conventional—and with which you are most comfortable. There is no exact recipe, no single right way to have a healing ritual. Rather, you must work with the ingredients you have at hand and put them together in ways that feel comfortable to you.

Here are some examples of healing rituals that other people have produced. They range from highly planned and structured ceremonies to more spontaneous events that only contain a few of the elements I've identified.

After Lynn was mugged in the big city and became fearful of going out, some of Lynn's fears and insecurities from early in her life were unearthed. When she was four years old, she had been taken from the security of her grandparents' farm to a major city. After this wrenching experience, she adapted to living without her grandparents. But the memory of them continued to be a source of security for her, representing the secure feeling that she would be taken care of and didn't have to live in fear. After her mugging, Lynn often felt the same feelings of insecurity that she had felt after leaving the farm.

Lynn made many changes after the mugging that contributed to her feeling safer. She began to make pilgrimages to her deceased grandparents' farm and eventually arranged for some of the other young people who also grew up there to join her. She renewed contacts with old friends and distant relatives from that early time of her life. During her visits, she spent long hours communing with the peaceful atmosphere of her childhood sanctuary. Here, a lot of Lynn's adult healing took place.

Lynn never defined what she was doing as performing a ritual. From her point of view, her traumatization had simply renewed her interest in her grandparents, the farm, and that period of her life. Making the trips and renewing old ties simply felt good and seemed to make sense. It's an excellent example of how we utilize informal rituals without realizing it.

Catherine was a young girl who was molested at a preschool. Her parents were very responsive to her fears and took many actions to help her feel more secure, but she and her parents remained preoccupied with the incident. Some of the older children were testifying in court against the accused molester, but despite being a mature four and a half Catherine was considered to be too young to be a credible witness. Her parents placed her in therapy, where she acted out the molestation a number of times. Though she didn't testify, the police did interview her and stayed in contact with her parents and therapist.

Catherine's difficulty moving beyond the trauma eventually led her mother to come up with the idea of doing a healing ritual for her. The policeman who had been talking to Catherine was asked to participate along with the therapist, the parents, and a social worker. The ritual consisted of a pretend trial in which the policeman would play the role of the judge, and Catherine would have the opportunity to testify. Catherine prepared for the trial by learning what happens in trials and what roles the judges, attorneys, and witnesses play. When the day of the "trial" arrived, Catherine approached the situation quite seriously. She knew it was not a real trial, but it was nevertheless a very important event for her. She asked to see the policeman's gun, which seemed to satisfy her that he had the proper authority.

The "trial" went very well; Catherine had her day in court. She talked openly about the molestation. The "judge" listened carefully and told her that he would take care of the "bad man." Catherine was worried that the "bad man" would be punished too severely, possibly fearing the revenge that molesters commonly threaten children with in order to keep them silent. The "judge" assured her that he already knew about this "bad man," that it wasn't only Catherine's testimony that was going to get him in trouble. The important thing was that he was going to see to it that the "bad man" did not hurt any more children. This seemed to satisfy Catherine. Afterward there was an air of relief, and she made greater progress in letting go of the traumatization.

This example contains the standard elements of a healing ritual. The power of the symbols of justice are worth noting. This four-and-a-half-year-old girl had already learned that policemen carry real guns as a symbol of their power. It's also noteworthy that this ritual was created almost entirely by the mother, though it required the participation of a number of outside "experts." This mother knew her daughter better than anyone else and understood what she needed in order to bring some closure to the trauma. Catherine continued to have to deal with what had happened to her, but her preoccupation with it changed after the "trial." It became a part of her past and no longer her whole life.

* * *

Karen, as an eight-year-old, lost her mother to an accidental death. Her father was a hardy person who was able to carry the family through the months following the death. Karen and Karen's younger brother busily pursued many activities with him in which he filled the role of their mother. But Karen's father discovered that there were some activities in which he simply could not replace their mother. One of these was Valentine's Day, when Karen frequently said that her mother used to make Valentine cards for her. Karen's father felt at a loss until he came up with the idea of having the family make a Valentine card and wreath and place it on the grave. Karen's father discovered that this ritual had a beneficial effect on the entire family, including himself.

This is just a small example of how we can use symbols, rituals, and memorials to help us get past traumatizations. When someone dies, life goes on for the survivors. But periodically, we encounter reminders that revive our feelings of loss, especially holidays and anniversaries. It's usually necessary to memorialize the loss on these days before we can experience them without being brought down by our memories. The stories of Catherine and Karen highlight the power of rituals to put a trauma to rest, "achieving closure." Rituals are especially important with children since they generally need to be able to perform actions in order to achieve closure. (Indeed therapy with children generally involves less talk and more action than therapy with adults.)

These rituals are fairly unstructured; not even the mock trial followed the rigid form we usually associate with rituals. The following structured ritual was specifically designed by the participants in order to get over a trauma.

Peter and Janice had been married for nearly fourteen years and had four children. Peter was a successful professional and a good provider. When they married, Janice had dropped out of law school in order to support Peter while he finished graduate school. She had hoped to return to school after Peter graduated and was working, but like many wives, she shelved the idea after she started having children. She didn't have great regrets about this since she found considerable satisfaction in being a homemaker.

After fourteen years, Janice discovered that Peter had been having affairs. She was traumatized by her discovery and felt that her sacrifices and her years of marriage had been wasted.

They entered marital therapy. Peter was contrite and acknowledged that he had hurt Janice and owed her. Still, their future as a couple was in doubt for some time. Eventually, Janice announced her desire to resume her schooling and finish her law degree. Peter showed his sincere desire to make up for what he'd done by cutting back to work part-time so that he could stay home with the children while Janice studied and attended classes. Within two years, Janice completed her degree and passed the bar. The family went on several trips together, and things seemed to be much better. But the trauma was not yet closed for Janice. She continued to find it difficult to be close to Peter, and she still felt the first fourteen years of their marriage had been ruined. She said she felt as though she would like to be divorced and married all over again so that they could start over with a "clean slate."

Janice didn't really want to put herself and her children through a divorce, but she did feel the need for some way to bury the past and start anew. Their therapist suggested creating a ceremony that might symbolize this transition without requiring the upheaval of a divorce. Janice enthusiastically responded to the suggestion, and Peter was willing, though initially he didn't think it would be any big deal. But as they decided what to do and then prepared for it, Peter discovered it was taking on a lot of importance for him as well. He ended up going to even greater lengths than Janice to find the appropriate symbols to include in the ceremony.

On the day of the ritual, Peter and Janice and their therapist went to the nearby shore of a lake. They first made a fire out of several things that Peter had brought, including an invitation to their wedding, several wedding pictures, and a broken frame containing the vows they had written for the wedding. The frame had been smashed by Janice during one of their fights following the discovery of the affairs. Interestingly, Peter had picked up the broken frame and saved it. After setting these things on fire, they kissed and each made a brief speech. Next they walked over to the water and threw their wedding bands into the lake (ouch). Again, they each made a brief speech about getting rid of the past and starting anew. They kissed, longer this time. They started holding hands as they walked and began acting downright giddy. Finally, they walked to a Dumpster and Peter placed a fancy jacket where any interested person could retrieve it. He had worn the jacket on his excursions with other women, and Janice was particularly pleased that he was getting rid of it.

Losses can't be relinquished until a certain amount of mourning has been done. A ritual can act as a catalyst to bring the mourning to the surface and create the opportunity for people to share in the experience. Peter had been growing sadder and sadder as the ceremony approached, and the prospect of throwing away their wedding bands made him feel as if he really had wasted those fourteen years. For the first time, he had begun to understand how Janice felt. And yet actually throwing away the bands proved to be very easy for both of them. It didn't make them sad—it released them from sadness.

By the time the ritual was over, Janice and Peter both felt unburdened. Indeed, Janice relinquished her preoccupation with Peter's broken vows. This powerful example of "cleaning the slate" with a ritual didn't occur until two years of work had been done, in which Peter changed his cheating ways, they both learned to communicate better, they processed what had happened, and Peter made major changes in his career to help Janice finish school.

Rituals are not magic—they can't fix everything in a single golden moment. But they *can* be a sort of peak experience in the larger process of recovery, which includes examining and processing the trauma, mourning the losses, dealing with symptoms, rebuilding a damaged sense of self, and rejoining society.

11

RESOLVING DEEP-SEATED BLOCKS
Working Through, Reconnecting, and Moving On

Some traumatized people have emotional blocks that prevent them from becoming involved with people on an intimate level, blocks that preceded the traumatization. And now they're interfering with the recovery. If these blocks are a part of who you are, they can be among the toughest impediments to your recovery and you may need to see a therapist to deal with them.

Problems with Guilt

You may find that your survivor guilt is particularly difficult to shed. Survivor guilt is often seen among people whose survival is, at most, only vaguely related to someone else's death. And even if your survival was clearly related to an-

other person's death, your guilt feelings have likely been influenced by other psychological issues besides the trauma.

People sometimes continue to have survivor guilt because it gives an illusion of having control: you could have
prevented the trauma if you'd only done a certain thing. This
attitude allows you to avoid the feelings of extreme helplessness that are part of the trauma. For you, the alternative to
feeling guilty may be high anxiety.

If we are already carrying guilt around with us, we're
more likely to respond to situations by feeling guilty. And a
propensity to feel unwarranted guilt can cause considerable
pain in our relationships. Consequently, we either avoid relationships or remain defensive within them. Feeling guilt for a
brief time helps us make moral choices in life; feeling excessively guilty hampers us and interferes with closeness.

People carry extra guilt for a variety of reasons. Some
people had parents or other significant adults who controlled
them by inducing guilt all the time. On top of feeling guilty,
these people are usually angry and likely to feel that others
are playing upon their guilt feelings. Other people feel excessive guilt for the opposite reason—they got away with too
much as children, felt they were taking advantage of their
parents' good nature, and developed a harsh attitude as a
way of controlling themselves. Children who are scared by
the intensity of the terrible anger they feel at parents and
siblings often learn to control themselves by feeling guilty.
Traumatization can bring any of these old guilty tendencies
to the surface. And the more guilt you feel, the less you'll be
able to engage in a trust relationship.

Excessive guilt is often manifested in self-blaming. As
you've seen, it's natural for you to question your behavior
and responsibility in the trauma. You go back over what happened hundreds of times and think about what you might
have done differently. But if you carried excessive guilt before the trauma, the natural process of self-examination can
turn into a destructive process of self-blaming. You must forgive yourself. If you think that what you've done is unforgiv-
able, try talking with someone who cares about you. You

might be surprised to find that someone else can understand and still accept you.

When Florence left her first husband to marry Barney, she lost custody of her three children—two boys and a girl—in the trial. There was a lot of animosity in the divorce, and the ex-husband subsequently made it very difficult for Florence to see her children. She was so upset by her loss that she went into a severe depression. The divorce took on a traumatic quality for Florence, and for years she was haunted by images of the judge announcing his decision to award custody to her ex-husband.

For several years, Florence had inconsistent, erratic contacts with her children. When Barney got a career opportunity in another city, they moved away. A year later, her middle child (and only daughter) became ill and died a few weeks after being diagnosed. Florence had not seen her before she died. After that, her ex-husband relaxed his hold a bit and started allowing the two boys to spend summers with Florence. When each boy finished high school, he went to live with Florence.

In her divorce, Florence had expected to be hurt financially, but she had never really considered the possibility that she could lose the custody battle. Despite her poor legal counsel, Florence got angry at no one but herself, and eventually Barney. She did not qualify for a diagnosis of Post-traumatic Stress Disorder, but she did have several of the symptoms. She withdrew socially and, from that time on, thought of her life in terms of before and after the divorce.

Then her daughter died. Florence subsequently became extremely overprotective with the boys. She made herself their personal slave whenever they were with her, and she and Barney frequently fought over Barney's desire to discipline the boys. Florence even blamed Barney for taking her away from her children because of his job—though she blamed herself even more. This theme underlay most of their fights.

Florence felt guilty about everything she'd done that resulted in her losing her children. She felt responsible for her daughter's death—even though she wouldn't have been able to change it had she been there. Her daughter's death stimulated trauma symptoms, such as emotional numbing, intrusive thoughts, sleep problems, and depression. Over time most of these symptoms improved, but her guilt continued. She had felt guilty before the child died, and the death only made her guilt heavier.

Only when Florence was able to share her feelings of guilt with Barney did they stop fighting. He had always felt that she blamed him, but when she talked about her own feelings of guilt, he saw that this was not the case. Still, the end of their fighting didn't mean Florence stopped feeling guilty. That only changed over time as Barney's consistent acceptance helped her look at herself from a new perspective.

Here are some things you can think about if you're suffering from excessive guilt:

- Did either of your parents ever express guilt? About what?

- Did you grow up in a judgmental atmosphere, where there was a rigid line between good and bad?

- Did people in your family apologize? Were apologies viewed as expressions of concern for others, or as a punishment for misbehavior?

- How quickly and sincerely were family members forgiven if they violated the family rules?

- Did you learn to forgive others? (If not, you may find it hard to forgive yourself.)

- Did you ever feel that other family members were trying to make you feel guilty in order to get their way?

- Did you grow up feeling that it was all right to be who you are or that what you are was not all right and that you must hide your innermost thoughts and feelings?

The answers to these questions can help you build a clearer picture of your background education and training in feeling guilty. Changing this picture means developing new rules. It can be very hard to change your family rules, but the first step is always identifying them. It's only then that you can decide what kind of rules make sense for the world you live in today. Here are some rules you might consider:

- Accepting responsibility for your own shortcomings should be applauded. This is a positive step in dealing with those shortcomings. You should feel good that you're dealing with them—not bad because you have them—and you should not use them as an excuse.

- The only person who can make you feel guilty is yourself. You must take other people's feelings into consideration, but ultimately *you* decide whether you're letting yourself down.

- An apology is a way of repairing a hurt. You do it because you care about the other person—*not* because someone must take the blame in order to stop the conflict.

- All feelings are acceptable. No one should be blamed or judged for having feelings.

Guilt is like the seasoning in a meal. A little bit makes everything better, but too much can ruin the food.

Difficulty with Loss

All trauma involves loss, whether it is an actual physical loss or an intangible loss such as the illusions of security. If you have a history of loss, then this can be a difficult issue for you. Many people who experience painful losses learn to protect themselves from having it happen again by trying to not get too attached to anything.

If your trauma was a major loss or if you have a history of loss, you may now find it difficult to let yourself get fully attached. You may play the game of fault-finding and maintain a defensive attitude toward the person with whom you're tempted to get close. You pull away and find reasons not to care—but since you're human, you do care. So you end up ambivalent, often attributing your own unhappiness to a fault in the person with whom you're involved rather than to your own fear of experiencing loss and hurt again.

Overcoming your fear of loss first means owning up to it. Once you accept that you're dealing with feelings of loss, it may be a little easier to see your aloofness as a way of staying away from those feelings. Perhaps you did not sufficiently mourn those other losses, and your current situation exacerbates feelings you already carried. But as you accept your need to mourn past losses and face your sadness, you will be able to invest in present relationships more easily.

Mourning loss is both a private and a shared experience. In the final analysis, you mourn alone, and part of what makes mourning so painful is the awareness of your basic aloneness. Yet paradoxically, you can begin to work through your loss by sharing the experience with others. Talking about a loss to a good listener can give words to your feelings and help you to understand them better yourself. Rituals enable you to communicate further with yourself and others and to crystallize feelings that are difficult to put into words.

Sean and Kelly suffered a traumatic loss and tried to live as if it didn't mean as much as it did. Their baby boy lived only four weeks. The loss was terribly traumatic for them, and they mourned for several months. Then they tried to resume their old lives, but they found it wasn't so easy. They developed problems in their marriage and argued a lot, and Sean started drinking heavily. Over the next several years, they grew even farther apart, and they stopped discussing when to have another baby. Sean became increasingly withdrawn, while Kelly became absorbed in doing volunteer work at a children's home. Additionally, Kelly began to take in every abandoned cat and dog that she came across and became active in an organization that cared for unwanted pets.

When Sean and Kelly were encouraged by a therapist to talk about the loss of "little Sean," they grew closer. They had each lived with their grief alone, each harboring secret feelings of guilt and blaming. Kelly was trying to be a successful mother to all the animals in town as part of her way of dealing with her guilt and replacing her loss. Sean was drowning his in the bottle. Even after these issues became clear, they continued to need professional help to work out the problems. Sean's alcoholism had become an independent problem and had to be treated. In addition, they both needed to grieve their loss.

Here are some questions for you to consider:

- What kind of losses do you have in your background? Have you lost dreams and opportunities as well as people?

- How was sadness treated in your family? Were all family members permitted to cry, or were there rules against some members showing sadness?

- How could you tell when your mother was sad? How about your father? Do you see any similarities with the way you behave now?

- What have you lost as the result of your traumatization?

And here are some things you can do:

- First of all, *talk* with your loved ones about your losses.

- Talk about the losses from earlier in your life as well as the current ones.

- Look at the ways that you've *denied* your losses by pretending that you didn't feel sad.

- Perform a ritual to help you acknowledge your loss. Get your loved ones involved in it.

- View yourself as in mourning, and give yourself time to feel your grief. Accept that you may be depressed for a while, but that it is appropriate.

- Say good-bye to those and that which you have lost.

History of Abandonment

Abandonment is related to loss—in fact, sometimes they're the same thing. But not always: You can be abandoned without actually losing the person. I'm talking about an *emotional* abandonment. If you have a heightened sensitivity to abandonment, it's likely you suffered either an important loss or an emotional disconnection from some significant caretaker in your childhood. You consequently carry feelings of insecurity now, and they increase when you find yourself becoming attached to someone.

Traumatization frequently stirs up abandonment issues, most obviously when there is a loss in the course of the trauma. But the link can be less direct. The simple fact that a traumatization has occurred can revive insecurities and fears that were formerly put to rest. Being traumatized places you in a more dependent state, even though you may resist it. And the more you feel you need other people, the more you're likely to reexperience concerns you had in previous situations where you relied on others.

As a child of eight, Irene was sent away to live with relatives for reasons that were never entirely clear to her. She departed under the impression that she would be returning to her parents' home within a couple of weeks, but it was several months before she came back. During the extended stay, she kept hearing that she would be going home shortly, but various things kept delaying her return. Her younger brother was still home and she talked to him and to her parents on the phone, always begging to be brought home as soon as possible.

She eventually returned, and the extended nature of her visit was never treated as a big issue. But as an adult, Irene developed fears of traveling and was overly protective of her children. In effect, neither she nor her family had ever acknowledged the traumatic effect that her extended "trip" as a child had had on her. But it left her with fears of being abandoned that were intense enough to influence her choice of husband and her approach to raising her children. Only after she examined these fears with a therapist did Irene begin to separate her childhood fears from the realities of her adult life. She was able to stop being overprotective and clingy with her children, and she became more comfortable with traveling.

If abandonment is an issue for you, the primary task is for you and your loved ones to be *aware* of your sensitivity to feelings of emotional abandonment. You should talk about your past feelings of abandonment. The more aware of them you are, the more you can separate the past from the present. Your loved ones can learn to be sensitive to these feelings and make efforts not to cause you to feel abandoned unnecessarily. But this means that you will have to speak up and let them know if you're feeling abandoned.

Difficulties with Rage

As we saw in Chapter 10, rage is a common consequence of traumatization. It is always difficult to deal with, but sometimes it can be terribly persistent—particularly when the traumatization uncovers rage from the past and unresolved issues from childhood.

Emmett was an upstanding citizen who was mistakenly accused of being involved in a major crime. He spent nearly four months in the county jail before the mistake was discovered and he was released. He was enraged, particularly at the police detective responsible for the case. Emmett had tried to explain to the detective that he couldn't have committed the crime, and he felt that the detective had not listened to him. After his incarceration, Emmett developed a number of symptoms of PTSD, including intrusive memories and dreams, social withdrawal, sleep problems, and angry outbursts. In the ensuing months, most of the symptoms improved, but Emmett had difficulty controlling his temper. He got into angry confrontations with the authority figures in his life, particularly his supervisors at work.

Emmett went to a therapist to get some help for his problems, particularly his angry outbursts. As he explored his feelings, he learned that the situation with the detective had revived feelings he had had about his father when he was a child. His father, a rigid disciplinarian, had beaten Emmett for minor infractions and had never listened to Emmett's side of the story. Emmett always felt that his father was unfair, but he learned to keep his anger to himself because it only led to more beatings. As an adult, Emmett avoided his old feelings of being treated unfairly by becoming a model citizen—until he was treated unfairly by the detective. Then Emmett lost trust in all men in positions of authority.

A clue to the childhood origins of Emmett's rage was what he said during confrontations with his supervisors: "You can't treat me this way, you're not my father." In therapy, however, he came to see the origins of this rage and developed the ability to separate that old anger from his current situation.

Damaged Sense of Self

Traumatization can cause you to revert to ways of dealing with life and coping mechanisms from earlier stages of your life. Psychologists call this phenomenon *regression*. If, as a child, you had difficulty maintaining an independent identity, you're at risk for developing similar problems following a traumatization. You may have had an overly protective parent who didn't allow you to make decisions or have independent feelings. Or perhaps your parent was too narcissistic and needed to be the center of attention, unable to allow you to have your own identity.

Parents aren't the only ones who contribute to such difficulties. Children can become excessively dependent upon an adult when they are lost in the shuffle of a large family or terribly outshined by a remarkable sibling, leading them to form a less independent identity. If you carry vestiges of such problems, traumatization can cause you to once more shy away from getting involved with others for fear of losing your independent sense of yourself.

Dale, who was traumatized by the abortion, is an example of someone whose old difficulties with her sense of self were uncovered by her traumatization. She had always lived her life for other people: She was the reliable friend to whom others turned, expecting her to take care of things. After her traumatic abortion, she developed a number of conflicts with her husband Ed. She felt taken for granted, and she argued with him that his needs always came first and that she was expected to be the one to do all the accommodating. When she explored this issue in psychotherapy, she found that she had always felt this way. Her family had placed much more importance on her brother than on her. They had encouraged his education, attended his athletic activities, and basically paid more attention to his needs. She had dealt with this situation by becoming the uncomplaining daughter and adoring sister, allowing her own interests to fade away.

Dale's traumatization brought these old issues to the surface. She felt that Ed had wanted the abortion for purely selfish reasons and that she'd gone along with it only to please him. This opened up a feeling in her that their entire relationship was structured to please him and facilitate his life. She just fit herself into the spaces he left her. As she uncovered her feelings about her family, her anger at Ed abated. She realized that she was most upset with herself for not taking more initiative in her life or pursuing her interests. She decided that this had to change. She went back to college and got the education that she'd always wanted. And as she took the initiative to make things happen in her life, her feelings about herself changed, and she no longer resented others for denying her opportunities.

If you're finding it difficult to maintain a strong sense of who you are, or if you fear being swallowed up by the other person in a relationship, the sanctity of a therapeutic relationship could help. I would recommend that you go into psychotherapy, especially if you don't have a good trust relationship. A professional therapist will protect your confidentiality and do everything possible to preserve your identity and sense of self.

Control Issues

One of the primary feelings that surfaces as a result of traumatization is helplessness. It's natural for anyone to try to avoid feeling helpless. And even if you grew up with more than your share of helpless feelings, you may have learned to cope by exerting control. We all use control to some extent. But some people become more strongly oriented than others toward controlling other people.

Manipulating and controlling produce different feelings on the part of the person being manipulated or controlled. Both kinds of behavior can make the person angry, but there are differences underneath that anger. When we've been manipulated, we feel *tricked,* and we tend to view the manipulator as dishonest or insincere. When we're controlled by someone else, however, we feel *helpless,* and we tend to view the controlling person as cold and uncaring. The manipulative person is trying to get something for himself, while the controlling person just needs to be in control in order to feel in control himself.

If you have control problems, you probably grew up in an environment that was chaotic or that contained someone who tried to control you excessively. You learned to cope with your environment by taking control yourself. Ironically, an overly controlling caretaker perpetuates the phenomenon by turning the child into yet another controlling parent.

Andrew had frequent battles over control with his wife, Lindy. The content of the conflicts often seemed much less important than Andrew's need to continually assert his control. He felt that Lindy couldn't be trusted to take care of things; he oversaw and double-checked everything she did. He was intellectual and practical, while she was fairly emotional. When they would get into an argument, he would come on very strong and insist that his point of view was the correct one. Lindy learned to back off, though she continued to resent his behavior. Andrew could not tolerate Lindy's emotionalism and would criticize her. As a result, Lindy felt controlled, and she said their conflicts made her feel as if he had "rolled over her with a steamroller."

When Andrew explored the issue of control in therapy, several things turned up in his past that helped explain his style. He had served in the air force in Vietnam and had been exposed to several rocket attacks at his base. He had shared a shelter with a group of men, and one particularly scared individual used to get the whole group spooked. Lindy's emotional arguments seemed threatening to him in the same way.

Further exploration revealed another emotional situation in Andrew's childhood. His father had left the family when Andrew was less than a year old, and his mother had focused all her attention on Andrew. He and his mother were very close for years, but he eventually came to feel suffocated by her excessive involvement with him. She tried to make all his decisions and told him what he was feeling. In order to fend her off, Andrew became controlling and intellectual— the same way he responded to the hysterical airman and his wife. He needed to control them because their emotional upheavals were too unsettling for him and left him feeling out of control.

Issues of Safety

If the trauma involves a physical threat, physical safety becomes a concern. Even a trauma that doesn't involve a physical threat can stir up safety issues from the past. If a trauma experienced in adulthood is severe enough, it can bring back the insecurity and fearfulness that you experienced in childhood.

In most of the examples in this chapter, an adult's traumatization has revived issues from earlier in life. But a trauma need not revive earlier issues to have a severe impact. Sometimes the nature of a particular traumatization is overpowering, and sometimes the recovery process is not allowed to take place. Penny was traumatized in her early twenties and, twenty years later, developed problems related to her inability to feel safe. There don't appear to have been any situations from her childhood that caused her to react this way. Rather, the trauma she experienced was so severe that her ability to feel safe at all was terribly mangled. Moreover, she had no opportunity to discuss and process the trauma.

Penny, as an independent and strong-willed girl, did well in school, was active in extracurricular activities, and was popular with her peers. She pursued activities—such as rock-climbing and sky-diving—that most people avoided. She learned to test her limits by trying new things and developed an attitude of competence and confidence in her own ability to deal with difficult situations. But after a traumatic incident in her second year of living on her own, this changed.

Penny became involved with a young man named David. He was close to his family and quite serious about the relationship with Penny. But some of David's traits bothered Penny, and she decided to break up with him. After the breakup, he called her repeatedly and pleaded with her to reconsider, and when she refused, he would often end the conversation with angry threats. One day, he convinced her to come by his place and pick up some things of hers that were still there. He told her he had accepted the breakup and was no longer angry. When she got there, he raped her, beat her up, and kept her in a room for approximately twenty hours. When his parents showed up unexpectedly, David was discovered, and they released Penny, treated her wounds and bruises, and pleaded with her not to tell anyone about the incident. They said that David was mentally disturbed and they were getting treatment for him and that he would be put away if the story were known.

Penny's traumatized condition made her particularly agreeable to doing as David's parents asked. After all, they had just saved her, treated her gently, and taken care of her. And she had always viewed herself as able to deal with very difficult situations without calling for help. So she agreed to protect David and keep the incident a secret. For many years she didn't talk about what had happened. But she was no longer the carefree, exuberant risk-taker that she'd been. She lived a quieter life, withdrew from her positions of high visibility, and adopted a blander image. She changed how she dressed, the kind of glasses she wore, how she wore her hair, and what she did with her free time. And she tried to forget those twenty hours during which she had feared being killed every moment.

Twenty years later, Penny married Charles, a reliable, even-tempered man who made her feel safe. Like Penny, Charles was familiar with all kinds of sports and adventurous activities, and they shared many interests. He had two grown children, a son and a daughter, who lived in another state. When Penny and Charles were around the son (whose name was also David), Penny felt that the young man was being disrespectful toward her. Some of his remarks even seemed hostile, and she asked Charles to speak to him. Charles felt she was overreacting and suggested she let it go. Over a period of several years, this pattern was repeated, and Penny's anxiety grew each time. She came to dread encounters with the son and was angry at Charles for minimizing her feelings and refusing to take her seriously.

Penny and Charles sought counseling for their marital problems. The most frequent dispute centered on Penny's anger that Charles would not reproach David.

As the intensity of Penny's feelings became clear to him, Charles began to realize that he had been unempathic to Penny. He accepted his responsibility to protect her and took a much firmer stance with his son. Only then was Penny able to unburden herself somewhat by talking about her trauma in therapy, and she processed it further by talking privately with Charles. Finally, they both discussed the situation with David, including Penny's traumatization. David apologized to Penny and became more sensitive in his dealings with her. Penny was still not the carefree risktaker she'd once been, but she found it easier to face fearful situations in her current life.

This chapter has focused on several kinds of issues that can be stirred up by traumatization. Many of them relate to the individual's personality and his or her approach to coping with life. These issues are representative of the kind of things that traumatized individuals often continue to work on after they've begun processing the primary trauma itself. There are certainly more issues than these, and every person's story is unique, but these are common ones.

Not only do these preexisting issues make recovery very difficult for trauma survivors, they also make life very difficult for the loved ones of trauma survivors. As a loved one, you're limited in what you can do because, to some degree, these issues themselves interfere with your attempts to explore them. If you try to talk with the trauma survivor about his guilt, you run the risk that he will experience you as blaming. Probing unresolved losses can provoke powerful reactions. The person who is sensitive to abandonment may feel abandoned every time she pushes you away. Trying to talk to your loved one about his rage is always risky. And it's easy to come on too strong with someone whose sense of self has been damaged. Trying to approach the issue of control with a controlling person is easily experienced as an attack and can turn into a control battle. And the underlying terror in the person who can't feel safe makes her distrustful.

So what can you do? The essence of what you can do comes back to what I've been stressing throughout the book. Develop a *trust* relationship. Talk about the feelings *between* you so that the air remains clear. You will only be able to discuss these and other difficult issues if you trust each other.

These issues are often resolved in psychotherapy. If you are the trauma survivor, you must decide whether to pursue psychotherapy. Your decision will depend upon the severity of your problem, the degree of your motivation, and the extent of your resources. But therapy can be tremendously helpful for the problems discussed in this chapter. The last chapter of this book will take you on a quick tour of the terrain of psychotherapy so that you may approach it with some degree of knowledge.

12

SEEKING PROFESSIONAL HELP

Finding the Right Therapist and the Right Treatment

Throughout this book, I have referred to the usefulness of psychotherapy for trauma survivors and their loved ones. Many of you who read this book will want to see a professional therapist to help you manage the recovery process and possibly root out deep-seated issues. So in this chapter, we will address the issue of finding an appropriate professional therapist. There are several factors to consider: the cost, the therapist's personal qualities, professional discipline, and theoretical orientation.

Cost

The cost of psychotherapeutic treatment varies according to the therapist's profession. Psychologists and psychiatrists in private practice are the most expensive. Social workers in private practice are less expensive but may still charge more than many clinics. Some clinics charge nearly as much as private practitioners, while others offer a sliding fee scale that is adjusted according to the patient's income. Some private practitioners also offer sliding scales. The more expensive private practice people are not necessarily better, but with them you'll have the most control over who you'll be seeing. In clinic settings, you're likely to be assigned to whoever has an opening.

One of the least expensive ways to get treatment is to go to a community mental health center. These are often subsidized by government funding and can afford to offer services below the going rate. Another good source of inexpensive treatment is a clinic that serves as a training facility. You'll likely be treated by a trainee, but this does not mean that you'll receive inferior therapy. If the facility is run responsibly, the trainees will be supervised by experienced therapists. Often you will receive good treatment here because of the extra time the trainee puts in discussing your case with a supervisor. But your therapist's fees and how experienced he or she is are only part of your evaluation. You should also be concerned with what kind of person your therapist is.

The Therapist's Personal Qualities

No one kind of therapist is best suited for everybody. But there may be a kind of therapist who is best for you. You are looking for a *good fit* between your therapist and yourself. Even a young, inexperienced therapist can be just right for you if you're comfortable with and have confidence in that individual. In the final analysis, you're looking for someone whom you can trust enough to let yourself be vulnerable. Remember, *you* make the final decision on whether to commit to this therapist or not.

But there are some general personal characteristics of therapists that make them better or worse for dealing specifically with traumatization, and so you should interview a potential therapist to determine whether he or she is right for you. (Here, for the sake of clarity, I will refer to the therapist as female.)

Acceptance of Traumatization as a Legitimate Problem

Believe it or not, some therapists don't "believe" in traumatization. Most of these "nonbelievers" think that only individuals with personality problems should be identified as having PTSD. They're not particularly interested in your trauma and may view it as an excuse for problems that were already there. So they downplay the need to talk about the trauma and focus instead on the current problems in your life or on your childhood. If your therapist doesn't believe in traumatization, then you probably won't get the kind of help you need. Find another therapist.

Many therapists who do believe in traumatization do not consider it important to talk about the trauma itself. Some feel that reliving the trauma retraumatizes the patient and doesn't contribute to recovery. They prefer to focus on the current situation. Clearly, I have a different view, but I respect their opinion. I have found that some people do not profit from extensive reexamination of the primary trauma. In any case, these therapists have different ideas from mine about how to be most helpful but they accept the premise that the traumatization is a legitimate problem.

Knowledge about Traumatization

The diagnosis of PTSD was developed only a decade ago, and many clinicians are not very familiar with it. Your therapist may know of the diagnosis but have little knowledge about the specific nature of traumatization. So ask her about her familiarity with PTSD. Lack of familiarity with a relatively new diagnosis is no sin, but she should be willing to acknowledge it. Does she have some idea what occurs in a case of traumatization and what needs to happen in order to recover from it?

After reading this book, your knowledge of traumatization and the recovery process should be relatively sophisticated. So don't be afraid to interview your prospective therapist. Your therapist doesn't need to be an expert in the treatment of PTSD, but should be open to recognizing the special aspects of the disorder. If she's open but not very knowledgeable about traumatization, give her this book to read and come back the following week.

Experience With Traumatization

Has she treated other people with trauma disorders? Has she had personal experience with traumatization? None of these is required to qualify the therapist, but the more experience she has had with traumatization, the greater the likelihood that she can help you with yours. Don't be afraid to ask her about it.

Personal Strength

What kind of person is this therapist? Do you get the feeling that she could stay connected with you in the midst of powerful, disturbing emotions? You can't tell a therapist's personal strength from her appearance, only from interacting with her. But ask yourself whether she seems to have the kind of strength of character upon which you can rely, even when you are experiencing something that will be very disturbing to *both* of you.

Capacity for Empathy

When you talk to this person, do you get the feeling that she really understands? Empathy is a necessary characteristic for all therapists, but some are better at it than others. The only way you can evaluate your therapist's empathic ability is by your own feeling. If you come away without feeling understood and supported, you may have a therapist who is not sufficiently empathic. Being empathic doesn't mean that the therapist will always agree with you, but it does mean that she's able to see and understand the situation from your point of view.

Capacity to Listen

The capacity to listen is closely related to empathy. It is what therapists are trained to do, and most do it very well. If you get the impression that your therapist is not listening carefully, it could be an indication of a problem. Good listeners can paraphrase what you are saying and demonstrate that they are following your thoughts. You must be able to tell your story and feel that your therapist listens well and understands how you see things. After the interview is over, ask yourself if you felt comfortable enough to tell your story. If not, something didn't work right. This is not necessarily cause to find another therapist, but it should be the first order of business for your next session.

Directness

As I have suggested, a significant trust relationship requires that the participants be able to discuss the feelings between them. Is your therapist going to be able to hold up her end of a trust relationship? In an initial interview, one indication you'll have is how she handles the questions you ask. Does she answer them directly and openly, or is she evasive? Bear in mind that the therapist has her own agenda for an initial interview and may be trying to get her own questions answered. So don't confuse evasiveness with the therapist's efforts to maintain control of the interview. Overall, however, did you feel that you were talking to a "real" person or to an actor who was hiding behind the role of professionalism?

A Consumer Orientation

Many people get so anxious when they first go to a professional therapist that they are more concerned with what she thinks of them than with what they think of her. It's all too easy to view the therapist as having all the answers while you take a sort of passive, obedient child role as the patient. But keep in mind that you are the consumer, and you are deciding whether to purchase this person's services. It's a very personal service, and the final decision is yours (although the therapist must also decide whether she can work with you). If you have a very positive feeling at your initial interview, you may make a decision at that time. But you may find it helpful to wait until you've had time to digest your impressions before you commit yourself.

Professional Disciplines

A number of different kinds of professionals perform psychotherapy. The primary ones are psychiatrists, psychologists, and social workers. In addition, a number of nurses with graduate degrees also perform therapy, as do other professionals who are trained therapists. Some renowned family therapists have been anthropologists, communications theorists, psycholinguists, and cyberneticists. I know family practice physicians and clergymen who have been trained to do family therapy. In fact, anyone can call herself a psychotherapist, since it is a generic label and not protected by law (in most states), like the label of psychologist.

So if you are uncertain about your therapist's credentials, ask about her training. Professional training is a must. All psychiatrists, psychologists, and social workers have professional training. Many people are uncertain about the differences among these disciplines, so here are some guidelines to help you.

Psychiatrists

Psychiatry is a medical specialty, just like surgery, orthopedics, and cardiology. Thus, all psychiatrists are physicians, and they hold the M.D. degree. All physicians must finish four years of medical school and pass medical board exams, then do residencies in their area of specialization. If your therapist is a practicing psychiatrist, she has completed a residency in psychiatry, usually consisting of a one-year internship and three years of residency training. Many psychiatrists perform fellowships and receive additional years of training, usually focused on some specific aspect of psychiatry. Some take their specialty board exams and are board certified in psychiatry. They're usually not required to be board certified to practice psychiatry, but it's expected for many official positions. If your psychiatrist displays her diplomas and certificates on the wall, you can learn a lot about her training by reading them.

Psychiatry training occurs in a hospital setting. Psychiatry residents are hospital staff members and are given primary responsibility for psychiatric patients in the hospital. As physicians, they're trained in the use of medications, and they can prescribe them as soon as they pass their medical boards at the end of medical school. So when they start their psychiatry residency, they are qualified as medical doctors even though they may have little or no experience with psychiatric problems. Usually, their experience is limited to a six-to-eight-week rotation on a psychiatric unit during medical school.

Psychiatrists are usually trained to do psychotherapy with a broad array of disorders, but since they're the only therapists who are also physicians, many of them get involved with the more severe cases—those requiring medications and hospitalizations. Most psychiatrists in private practice are on the attending staff of a hospital. If you are receiving medications for psychiatric symptoms, a psychiatrist should always be involved. Other physicians are qualified to prescribe medications for psychiatric conditions, but you're better off being monitored by a trained psychiatrist who is familiar with these particular drugs and their effects.

Psychologists

There are a number of subareas in psychology, but it is *clinical* psychology that constitutes the training of the bulk of practicing psychologists. In order to be called a psychologist in most states, the individual must meet various qualifications, including supervised experience in a year-long internship. But the nature of a psychologist's degree can vary, and individuals with degrees in other areas of psychology can usually be licensed as psychologists as long as they get the clinical internship training. Most graduate programs in psychology provide several years of training prior to the internship. But this varies with different schools and programs. Some place a greater emphasis on clinical training than others. Many psychologists receive further (usually more specialized) training in postdoctoral fellowships, performed in hospitals or clinics.

The degrees that psychologists hold can be confusing. Some have master's degrees, but most have doctorates—either Ph.D.'s, Ed.D.'s, or Psy.D.'s. The Ed.D. is from a department of education and is usually in counseling psychology. The Psy.D., a newer degree, is granted by programs that are oriented toward producing professional clinicians (as opposed to academics or researchers). The Ph.D., the more traditional academic degree, requires proficiency in research and scholarship. Thus, if your psychologist has a Psy.D., you can assume that her education had a strongly clinical orientation. If she has a Ph.D. or an Ed.D., she may have attended a program that emphasized scientific skills over clinical skills, but this is becoming less and less common as most programs now focus on both.

The clinical training of psychologists includes psychological assessment (the use of such tools as intelligence and inkblot tests) as well as psychotherapy. Whereas psychiatry education is focused on illness, psychology training is focused more on studying how the human personality functions. That's why the personality tests that psychologists use are designed to tap into the basic processes that make up the personality. Clinically, psychologists strongly emphasize learning, and they tend to consider medication less often than psychiatrists.

Social Workers

The field of social work evolved as an applied profession, rather than as an area of academic study like psychology. Social workers correct sociological problems at the grass roots and help people who are having problems make the best use of societal resources. Most social workers have a master's degree—the M.S.W.—which fully qualifies them to practice. A doctoral degree in social work usually does not add more clinical training; rather, it emphasizes research and scholarly skills. There are different specialties in social work, some of which are oriented toward administrative skills and offer no clinical training. The social workers who are therapists have generally been trained in psychiatric social work, though it may be labeled differently at different programs.

Social workers usually receive one to two years of clinical training in clinics or hospitals. They often put a stronger emphasis on client advocacy and social issues than psychologists or psychiatrists. They are licensed in most states and can operate independently. Many states used to require that social workers be supervised by a psychiatrist, but these days, social workers are recognized as competent professionals who do not need to be supervised by another discipline.

Social workers are trained to look at the individual

within the community. To make a gross oversimplification, we might say that where the psychiatrist looks for disease and the psychologist looks at the personality, the social worker looks at the individual's situation. Social workers are more likely to work with the family, the school, and other community resources.

I should note here that there are more similarities than differences among these three disciplines. Psychologists and psychiatrists certainly do not ignore the individual's situation, and social workers are well aware of psychiatric disorders.

Before I leave the topic of professional discipline, I should reveal my own background so that you can evaluate my biases. I am a psychologist, and I hold a Ph.D. in clinical psychology. I received three years of training before my internship, two years of internship, and another year of postinternship training. The three years of preinternship training were part time, as I was attending classes at the same time. All my training took place in hospitals and clinics associated with hospitals, since I attended the clinical psychology program at Northwestern University Medical School.

Theoretical Orientations

As you may or may not know, therapists have different theoretical orientations. In this section, I will give you a brief overview of the different theoretical approaches. Among the many theories of human behavior, these are some of the ones that are most often employed in treating traumatization.

Behavioral Approaches

Behaviorists do not relish theories that invisible forces are operating inside the psyche. Rather, they focus on what can be measured and observed in people's behavior. In a classic behavioral experiment, Pavlov trained dogs to associate the ringing of a bell with being fed. They would then salivate upon hearing the bell—the dogs were "conditioned" to respond this way by the conditions in which were fed. Behaviorists look for the ways in which people, too, are conditioned to maintain certain behaviors. Of course, they focus on more sophisticated rewards than being fed, but the principle is the same. A behavioral approach focuses on changing a person's external environment in order to change his behavior. With humans, the external environment refers to a number of things, including other people's responses to the person.

Behaviorists may try to change the way you respond to your memories of the primary trauma through such devices as the desensitization techniques described in Chapter 9. Most behaviorists would also work on changing your current symptoms by helping you alter your environment. Some behaviorists also work with the family, again trying to help people work out problems by altering the ways they respond to each other. I think behavioral approaches are most useful in dealing with some of the physical symptoms that accompany traumatization. Other issues, such as the survivor's loss of meaning, seem to be less responsive to behavioral methods.

Cognitive Approaches

Cognitive approaches focus on how and what people think; their goal is to develop more rational thought. Some people are more responsive to this approach than others. I think people who are more intellectual can make the best use of this approach. It can be useful with issues like self-esteem (as we have seen in Chapter 10) and obtaining a more balanced perspective on the primary trauma, but it doesn't seem to work in isolation. In order to make use of cognitive tools, you need to feel supported emotionally. Thus, cognitive approaches for traumatization work best when they're accompanied by a supportive trust relationship.

Family Systems Therapy

The theory underlying most family therapy approaches is called *systems theory*. Its premise is that the behavior of an individual cannot be understood in isolation but must be looked at from the perspective of how it fits into the entire family system. An apparent problem in one family member may actually be serving a function for other family members. For instance, a child with a behavior disorder may serve to take the heat off of the parents' marital problems. Or a wife's depression may serve to help her husband overcome his low self-esteem and feel better about himself by taking care of her. Family therapists typically see individuals with problems in the company of their spouses or families.

There are a number of schools of family therapy, combining systems theory with practically every other theoretical approach. Family therapy is a powerful tool in the treatment of traumatization because it allows therapists to influence those important trust relationships in the family (where most recovery takes place). Sessions with the family can help trauma processing take place and help the family remove any blocks against that processing. But if the traumatization is downplayed and erroneously viewed as an attempted solution for some other family problem, a family therapist can fail to acknowledge the importance of the trauma.

Family therapy means being in therapy with your spouse or lover, with your children, your parents or your whole clan, or any combination of the above. The therapy will inevitably deal with your relationships with one another, even if the problem that brings you there is associated with only one family member. The therapy may be quick and focused on how to help that symptomatic member, or it may be focused on family problems that are related to the individual member's symptoms. Usually, families with traumatized members make use of family therapy to break down barriers and open the kind of communication I advocate in Chapter 6.

Psychodynamic and Psychoanalytic Approaches

Therapists who practice psychodynamic and psychoanalytic approaches are primarily interested in the internal processes of the individual and how those processes are manifested in relationships. Change is to be brought about by developing *insight,* wherein the patient comes to understand the hidden reasons underlying his behavior. Psychoanalysis has the largest body of theory of all psychological approaches and is sometimes criticized because of its strong reliance on theory.

Psychoanalysis refers to both a theory and a technique that the psychoanalyst uses. In its purest form, psychoanalysis involves lying on a couch and free-associating with a therapist several days each week. The therapist is called an analyst, and her job is to analyze the psyche of the patient. Only in true psychoanalysis is the therapy conducted in this way, however. Most psychoanalytic therapists are not analysts (it requires additional training) and do not offer psychoanalysis per se. Rather, they use psychoanalytic theory to help their patients achieve insight, but they have modified the classic (Freudian) psychoanalytic method. They see patients less frequently—usually once or twice each week—and may be considerably more active, directive, and supportive than the classic method prescribes.

The psychoanalytic approach pays considerable attention to the lifelong effects of early childhood experiences, reasoning that current problems often relate to childhood experiences, such as the deep-seated blocks we examined in Chapter 11. The primary criticisms of the approach are that insight does not necessarily produce change and that the treatment process is unnecessarily slow. Psychoanalytic practitioners argue that problems take a long time to develop and that lasting change is equally difficult to develop. Although the critics are right that insight does not always lead to change, the psychoanalytic counterargument is that insight allows the individual the *choice* to change. Doing it is still up to the individual.

Clinicians have applied psychoanalytic theories and methods to traumatization. Psychoanalytic theories help explain many aspects of traumatization, and this book is founded on some of those theories. My only caution about the psychoanalytic approach is that the clinician must be aware of or willing to learn about the unique aspects of traumatization. If a clinician views traumatization as only a minor vehicle for unearthing childhood issues, she is making the same mistake as the family therapist who discounts the trauma in favor of family system pressures. Very often, I find that traumatization does unearth childhood issues, but the overwhelming nature of the primary trauma requires that it be dealt with first and, once it is dealt with, the childhood issues often become irrelevant. Sometimes, however, as in the examples from Chapter 11, deep-seated problems become the new focus for therapy as the traumatization is resolved.

Eclecticism

I've described several approaches and emphasized some of their differences. Some people practice these approaches in purer forms than others. Those who take bits from one approach and pieces from another—and refuse to be categorized by only one—refer to themselves as eclectic. Most therapists are influenced by more than one approach but may accept one label as generally descriptive of how they operate. Thus, a clinician may call herself psychoanalytic, yet help parents employ behavioral strategies in dealing with their child's misbehavior.

Brief Psychotherapy

In brief psychotherapy, treatment is focused on a few specific goals and is conducted with a time limit, such as twelve or twenty sessions. The therapy may rely upon the theories from any of the other approaches; it is simply limited in what it targets. In brief psychotherapy there tends to be a very efficient use of the time and a lot of goals can be achieved. The format doesn't lend itself well to *vague* goals; the more specific the goals are, the more likely they'll be achieved. Thus, it is not the best approach to use to pursue total recovery from traumatization, but it can be very helpful for pursuing specific goals that are *part* of that recovery. Many insurance plans provide for only brief psychotherapy by covering something like twenty sessions per year. If you pursue a time-limited therapy, be sure to set realistic goals so that you don't frustrate yourself and come away feeling that therapy can't help.

Group Psychotherapy

Group psychotherapy is therapy with a group of strangers, sometimes for a fixed period of time, such as twelve sessions. Groups are an unusual kind of treatment because some of the most significant influence comes from the other group members—other patients—rather than from the professional therapist. Groups can be a tremendous source of support, particularly if you have become socially isolated. The best type of group for people who have been traumatized is a group of other people who have been traumatized. Traumatized people may feel less alienated if they can relate to others who have been through similar experiences. The national network of Vet Centers has run groups for traumatized veterans for the past decade. Many veterans have found this to be their lifeline and the beginning of their journey back.

Again, I should share my own orientation and approach so that you know my biases. I operate according to a mixture of psychoanalytic and family systems approaches, with a little behavioral technique thrown in. I place a premium on the development of insight, whether with families or individuals. For people recovering from trauma, I place a premium on support and the opportunity to share the burden. Much of what I do is what I have advised you to do in this book, and my job is often devoted to removing the blocks that are preventing patients from doing their jobs.

I, of course, leave it to you to decide whether you need to see a professional therapist. If you're uncertain, go for a session and see what emerges. Many people go into therapy and find themselves crying and getting emotional about things that they didn't think they had a lot of feelings about. If you do go to a therapist to deal with your own or your loved one's traumatization, be sure to consider the personal qualifications of the therapist. Find a good fit. Trust your gut feeling about your therapist. Be open—talk with her about your feelings about her and how she conducts your therapy. Therapy is not something that a therapist does to you; it is something you do together.

AFTERWORD

You now have a picture of the trauma response, including the variety of ways in which the trauma survivor and his loved ones can suffer and the ways in which they all can recover. I've drawn a map for recovery; whether you've personally been traumatized or are the loved one of someone who's been traumatized, the map can help you recognize what you're looking for and, I hope, get there sooner.

I've emphasized the importance of processing the trauma and tried to show how, if you are a trauma survivor, you can use your relationships with people who care about you to help you process it. Although processing is an internal event, it's stimulated by external events, particularly by examining your feelings and attitudes with someone you trust. Processing may take quite some time, for you're coming to terms with a new view of yourself and your world. But there may be moments, particularly those that occur with the catalyst of a ritual, in which your new worldview can evolve abruptly. I've pointed you toward some of the rituals that are already available to you and suggested ways you can develop your own rituals.

As you process the trauma, its meaning can change for you. And as its meaning changes, it can lose some of its prominence in your mind and become a part of your past, instead of your present. While this may release you from your domination by the trauma, it may not change many of the negative things that have happened in your life as a result of your living with traumatization. Along with processing your traumatization, you must take actions to improve other aspects of your life as well. You must attend to your physical health, your life-style, and your self-esteem. Any of these can bog down your progress in processing your traumatization.

My Interest in Trauma

I grew up in Dallas and was a senior in high school in November 1963, when John F. Kennedy flew to Love Field Airport that fateful Friday. I arranged to be off from school to join the many young people who greeted his plane at the airport. President Kennedy refused to go right to his car—he insisted on walking over to the fence and shaking hands with some of the people in the crowd. I shook hands with the President of the United States, and half an hour later he was killed by an assassin in my home town.

Like so many people in this country, I felt that loss as if he had been a member of my family. I went through a trauma response—years of coming to think of the world in a different way. It was no longer the safe world I had lived in up until then. After Kennedy's assassination, there followed a series of assassinations of famous people, and before the 1960s were over, many people had lost their sense of security and were angry that they didn't feel safe. The values of American society lost their meaning for a lot of people during that period.

One of the things I did to deal with it all was joining the Marine Corps during the Vietnam War. Boot camp has a way of giving life meaning *very* quickly. I lived through several traumatic events in Vietnam; the worst was the loss of my closest friends. I lived another trauma response of many years' duration after I returned from Vietnam.

At the worst of my traumatization following Vietnam, I was emotionally numb to almost everything. Sleep problems, particularly recurring nightmares, haunted me. I was very lonely and cut off from people. I felt different because of the war, and I was still trying to figure out what I believed. I listened to both sides of the war controversy and didn't know who was right. I knew I wanted it to end, that I didn't want any more people to die. I looked for answers. I searched through philosophy, tried to express myself by writing poetry, and struggled to figure what I was going to do with myself.

In the 1970s, I stumbled into the field of mental health, seeking help as much as offering it. I worked for six and a half years at a residential facility for children and adolescents. That place, the Oaks Center of the Brown Schools in Austin, was my recovery environment. It was like a healthy family—stable, expressive, supportive, tolerant, and wise. My friends and my work there helped me put the meaning back into my life. My family in Dallas was also supportive and tolerant of the many years I took to get my life together.

I know many veterans like myself who healed during the 1970s. Unfortunately, many more have yet to settle in with a healthy family. But more than the veterans were traumatized by the Vietnam War (and perhaps because it was on the heels of Kennedy's assassination)—I think the whole country was traumatized by it.

Of course, a lot of people did much to try to deal with the trauma of the war, but taken as a whole, I think the entire country was affected and lived through a trauma response that wasn't really healed until the veterans were welcomed home in the 1980s. That may have been too late for some of them, but I think the country itself needed to do it as badly as the veterans needed it. Welcome home parades are part of our natural healing from wars.

You've probably read this book because of a particular trauma that you or a loved one has suffered. Now you have the chance to put what you've read to work. Of course, every trauma is different, but the pattern of a trauma response is basically the same. It may vary in intensity, duration, and symptoms. But underlying it all, someone's worldview has

been shaken, and they need time and support while they re-
build it. It's up to you to apply the principles of recovery to
your particular situation.

I wish you the best of luck in your recovery work. I've
suggested many concrete things that you can do, but only the
rituals were purely symbolic. I can't promise to answer your
letters, but I would love to hear about the rituals that you
find most helpful. You can write to me to tell me about them
at:

> The Phoenix Institute
> 445 E. Ohio, Suite 410
> Chicago IL 60611

When I was a boy, I saw a tree blasted by lightning. It
split down the middle, then lay in two great halves on the
ground. It went down in the spring, but some of the leaves on
the tree stayed green into the fall. The tree was refusing to
die, although I assumed that its death was inevitable. Late in
the fall, the park service came and cut the dead parts away
from the tree, but they left a section of the trunk that was still
alive. My friends and I played on the trunk of the tree, giving
no thought as to why they would leave it on the ground still
attached to the roots.

The next spring, I discovered a sapling growing straight
up out of the roots, tall and strong. It looked like a limb, but I
guess it was a new trunk. It grew over the years into a large
tree with a strange little section that grew out near its base.
The tree had survived. It didn't survive the way I would have
predicted (but the park service must have known what they
were doing).

If you walk through a grove of trees and look closely,
you'll see many signs of the traumas they've endured—places
where limbs have been lost, where trunks had to angle to
accommodate an obstacle. If you look at the tree's rings,
you'll see the years when water was scarce and the tree had
to restrict its growth. Similarly, there are people around you
who've been through traumas—*many* more than you might

think. The signs of trauma are there with the people as well, but they're less obvious. You have to talk with them to determine if they've had to heal over a place where something was lost, or grow in a new direction in order to deal with some obstacle.

Every one of those people has experienced their trauma response in their own particular way, just as you and your loved ones must deal with your particular traumatization in your own way. But the better you understand the territory you're in, the better your chances of finding your way through it. Now you have a map.

Good navigating!

APPENDIX

Resources

For Further Reading

There are a number of books available for those readers who wish to pursue further reading in specific areas. Here are some books that are frequently recommended:

For survivors of sexual abuse:
The Courage to Heal by E. Bass and L. Davis (New York: Harper and Row, 1988).

For parents:
No More Secrets: Protecting Your Child From Sexual Assault by C. Adams and J. Fay (San Luis Obispo, CA: Impact, 1981).

For survivors of loss:
How to Survive the Loss of a Love by M. Colgrove, H. Bloomfield, and P. McWilliams (New York: Bantam, 1976).

For survivors of suicide:
After Suicide by J.H. Hewett (Louisville, KY: Westminster John Knox, 1980).

For survivors of child abuse:
Outgrowing the Pain: A Book for and About Adults Abused As Children by E. Gil (San Francisco: Launch Press, 1983).

For survivors of dysfunctional families:
Healing the Child Within: Discovery and Recovery for Adult Children of Dysfunctional Families by C.L. Whitfield (Deerfield Beach, FL: Health Communications, 1987).

For survivors of sexual assault/rape:
I Never Called it Rape by R. Warshaw (New York: Harper and Row, 1988).

For survivors of divorce:
Rebuilding: When Your Relationship Ends by B. Fisher (San Luis Obispo, CA: Impact, 1981).

For children in divorced families:
The Boys and Girls Book About Divorce by R. Gardner (New York: Bantam, 1971).

For survivors of Holocaust families:
Children of the Holocaust: Conversations with Sons and Daughters of Survivors by H. Epstein (New York: Putnam and Sons, 1979).

For survivors of the Vietnam War:
Shrapnel in the Heart: Letters and Remembrances from the Vietnam Veterans Memorial by Laura Palmer (New York: Random House, 1987).

For family members of Vietnam veterans:
Recovering From the War: A Woman's Guide to Helping Your Vietnam Vet, Your Family, and Yourself by P.H.C. Mason (New York: Penguin Books, 1990).

For sleep problems:
Sleep Problems and Solutions by Q. Regestein, D. Ritchie, and the Editors of Consumer Reports Books (Mount Vernon, NY: Consumers Union, 1990).

For meditation:
The Relaxation Response by H. Benson (New York: Avon, 1975).

For stress management:
The Relaxation and Stress Reduction Workbook by M. Davis, E.R. Eshelman, and M. McKay (Oakland, CA: New Harbinger, 1982).

For anger management:
The Dance of Anger by H.G. Lerner (New York: Harper & Row, 1985).

For alcohol/drug problems:
I'll Quit Tomorrow by V. Johnson (New York: Harper & Row, 1980).

For eating problems:
Feeding the Hungry Heart: The Experience of Compulsive Eating by G. Roth (New York: Signet, 1982).

For the professional who wants to learn more about traumatic stress, I highly recommend a series of books produced by Brunner/Mazel called the Psychosocial Stress Series, as well as the *Journal of Traumatic Stress* (Plenum Press), a quarterly publication that provides the best articles on the nature and treatment of traumatization.

Both the journal and the book series are associated with the International Society for Traumatic Stress Studies, 435 N. Michigan Avenue, Suite 171, Chicago, IL 60611-4067. Phone: (312) 644-0828; fax: (312) 644-8557. The Society has also produced a curriculum for professionals interested in working with post traumatic stress disorder. It can be ordered from the society. The title is:

The Initial Report from the Presidential Task Force on Curriculum, Education, and Training by Y. Danieli and J.H. Krystal (1989).

Helping Resources

Aside from the support services offered by your own community and clergy, here are some other resources that you might want to look into:

Vet Centers

These neighborhood mental health centers are run by the Department of Veterans Affairs Readjustment Counseling Service to aid veterans, particularly those who are suffering from war stress. There are nearly two hundred at this writing, all run by people devoted to helping veterans. Check local listings for the center nearest you.

Survivors' Groups

If you've been victimized and don't have a good support system, it is worth your while to find a support group such as those listed below. The people who run these organizations will have an appreciation for what you've been through.

AA World Service (Alcoholics Anonymous), P.O. Box 459, Grand Central Station, New York, NY 10163, (212) 686-1100. Check local listings as well.

Al-Anon Family Group Headquarters and *Alateen* (both for the families of alcoholics), World Service Office, P.O. Box 862, Midtown Station, New York, NY 10018–0862, (212) 302-7240. Check local listings as well.

Group Project for Holocaust Survivors and Their Children, 345 East 80th Street, New York, NY 10021, (212) 737-8524.

Incest Survivors Anonymous, P.O. Box 5613, Long Beach, CA 90805, (213) 422-1632.

National Association for Children of Alcoholics, 31582 Coast Highway, Suite B, South Laguna, CA 92877, (714) 835-3830.

National Child Abuse Hotline, Childhelp USA, (800) 4-A-CHILD.

National Coalition Against Domestic Violence, P.O. Box 15127, Washington, DC 20003–0127, (800) 333-7233.

If you can't find what you're looking for in the listings above, the following organizations will try to put you in touch with the right group in your area:

Alliance of Information and Referral Services (AIRS), P.O. Box 3456, Joliet, IL 60434. (Send a stamped self-addressed envelope to receive a list of support groups in your area).

National Organization for Victims Assistance (NOVA), 1757 Park Road, NW, Washington, DC 20010, (202) 232-6682.

National Self-Help Clearinghouse, 25 West 43rd St., Rm. 620, New York, NY 10036, (212) 840-1259.

INDEX